Business Ethics of our Fathers

Note – synagogue in Budapest, Hungary (top) and New York City, New York / USA.

Table of Contents

I. Introduction - from Bereshit to Bernie Madoff

Business ethics is an extremely important topic that encompasses the methods in which employers treat employees, employees treat employers, consumers treat sellers, and buyers treat suppliers. Textbooks have included stories of various ethical scandals, such as inventory scandals dating from the 1930s and inflated revenue issues in the 1980s. Some of the most pernicious scandals occurred in the late 1990s / early 2000s included the fall of Enron, WorldCom, Arthur Andersen and other companies. After the scandals in the 1990s/early 2000s, the business world seemed to focus more on ethical issues. Business schools increased the focus on ethics. As the Enron scandal was, in large part, an accounting scandal (the scandal destroyed one of the largest and oldest accounting firms, Arthur Andersen), the accounting field also changed. In order to maintain the CPA license, accountants must take ethics training in many states. The US government created and passed the Sarbanes Oxley Act, increasing responsibility of corporate Board of Directors, creating harsh new penalties, and requiring executives to take accountability. Corporate Social Responsibility became an important topic, as businesses are voluntarily measured the ability to help the community - and not just the bottom line.

Despite new regulations as well a focus on Corporate Social Responsibility (CSR) and "accountability", ethical scandals continued throughout the 2000s and 2010s – the housing bubble and questionable loans, Bernie Madoff defrauding investors, Snowden providing information about the NSA, and the GSA (USA federal agency) conference scandal. Large corporations, small businesses, federal agencies, banks, state and local entities and individuals acted in short-sighted and selfish ways.

Judaism teaches many important stories about business ethics. The stories are from books written millennia ago, books written (or orally transmitted) hundreds of years ago, books written in the past few years, and recent Rabbis' sermons. The stories and laws provide important insights today, and will likely provide helpful guidance tomorrow.

The Hebrew Bible (known to many as the "Old Testament") provides numerous important stories that provide some insights and guidance on business ethics. Humans made questionable ethical choices from the very beginning. Rabbis had segmented the Torah (the first five books of the Bible) into sections for each week. In temples, Jews read a section (parsha) on Saturday. The first parsha is called Bereshit, from the Hebrew phrase for "In the Beginning". Bereshit demonstrates many examples of what not to do – a snake encourages Eve to eat an apple from a tree, though G-d had requested that Eve not eat from the Tree. Eve does not obey G-d's request (insubordination). When G-d had requested the reason Adam ate from the Apple, Adam stated that it was due to Eve (not taking responsibilities for his/her action). G-d punishes Eve and Adam by abolishing them from the Garden of Eden, forcing them to suffer numerous other punishments, such as forcing Adam to work with the sweat of his brow.

Rabbis who lived after the Bible provided numerous interpretations of the Bible. Parts of the Bible, especially the Torah, contain relatively few words to describe hundreds of years of history or monumental events. Rabbis have provided interpretations of the Torah. The interpretations were a mixture of stories inspired by the Bible (in some cases, the stories could "fill in the blanks" of narrative not included in the Bible), as well as various rules. Many of the rules in the Bible and interpretations from the Rabbis were for commerce. The Bible, Talmud, and other works contain numerous rules, guidelines and ideals relating to commerce – buying, selling, managing, and working. Stories from the Bible are thousands of years old, while Rabbis' interpretations were written centuries ago written. Back then, there was no internet, TV, radio, cars, or the Dow Jones. Yet, the Hebrew Bible and other books have much to teach us about running, owning, and analyzing a business.

As one of my study partners has noted, one of the major differences between much of modern society (at least recently), was a focus on rights versus responsibilities. Modern society often focuses on rights, while the Rabbis focus on responsibilities, including the responsibilities that businesses had for providing employees. Therefore, this book will focus on the responsibilities of employees, employers, vendors, and customers. We have a responsibility to act in a way to help others

In fact, so often regulations have focused on the rights of employees, vendors, consumers, etc. Too many laws are created and too many employee lawsuits are initiated because employers sometimes did not think about responsibilities to vendors, employees, and the community. At the same point, employees sometimes do not truly consider basic responsibilities to employers. Employees sometimes take as much as they can and work as little as possible. Employers sometimes demand too much and pay too little, and often provide no reasonable road to financial success. If employees and employers think about what they owe to each other, we can have a superior situation for everyone involved.

While some of the rules in this book are simple and straightforward (e.g., paying employees promptly), others are not. Other rules are frankly different than the common business practices. For example, the rules include not overcharging consumers for goods, or to not underpay. In addition to guidelines to specific situations or topics, it is also important to consider overall ethical principles.

II. Approach

A book that would provide all major Jewish business rules, modern regulations/rules, and recent business news stories would be too long and too detailed. The book could be extremely large, and contain very long technical rules. Instead, this book will provide guidance for ethical situations, providing many brief though key lessons.

III.   Importance of Business Ethics

Jewish interpretations of laws recognized the importance of ethics many years before corporate social responsibility, Enron and the SEC.

In the bible, after G-d provided the Torah to the Jews (Exodus 18:1-20:23), the very next section (parsha) is *Mishap Tim*, which "contains the laws of damages and guideline for" a court (the *Beis Din*. Reasonably, after the Lord provided the important mission to the Jewish people, the Lord asked the Jewish people to "immerse themselves in prayer and offerings." Instead of focusing on ritual prayer, the next section (Exodus 18:20-24) teaches about "financial dealings". The logic is that a step in the journey from Sinai to Israel was to ensure that "interpersonal dealings" measure up to "Judaism's standards. Only after the Jews mastered appropriate behavior between fellow Jewish could they advance to the next stage of service to Hashem [G-d]." This instructs the reader of the importance of dealing with others[i]. The Torah (first five books of the Bible) contains 613 rules ("direct commandments"). Of the 613 commandments, over 100 are for commerce. [ii]Hence, the importance of the business ethics is very high on the list of ethical pronouncements.

Why Does Business Matter?

In other religious traditions, wealth is not seen as a good thing; in some cases, clergy take a vow of poverty. Judaism does not have such guidance. Wealth can potentially be used as a means to help society. Following quote and interpretation puts it best:

> "Rabbi Elazar ben Azaryah said, "**Where there is no money, there is no learning**." This is a literal translation, but the rabbis expanded it to mean that unless people's stomachs are full, they cannot study, grow spiritually, or do good deeds." [iii] (Author's bold)

This remains true today; it can be hard to perform good deeds and health others if one does not have proper food and shelter, or is otherwise struggling financially.

IV.   Justice v. Just Profit

The Jewish legal texts (Halachah) often focus on justice. Justice encompasses proper dealings in business; Justice includes charging reasonable (market-based) prices, paying workers on time, truly giving the job promised to a perspective employee, and other important matters of fairness.

In the capitalist society, one school of thought is that profit is far more important than any other goal. Finance professors often taught that the main point of a business is increasing owner (shareholder) wealth - other goals of helping the environment, promptly paying employees, increasing the number of employees, or providing the best products were seen as lower priority. While there has been a recent focus (at least companies seem to claim) in Corporate Social Responsibility or sustainability, in actuality, companies have continued making steps to increase the owner wealth instead of other goals.

In the late 1990s, one business executive said that there is not truly any business ethics. Instead, businesses do whatever they can do that would not get the businesses caught or into trouble.

A. Consumer Responsibilities

1. Value Everyone's Time – Don't Ask Vendors the Price if You Have No Intention of Buying

While children will not join the workforce for many years, children will actually participate in commerce very early in their lives. Children will go into stores, and be able to purchase goods, (e.g., toys). One of the simplest, yet effective rules is the guidance to not ask someone the price of the product, if the child simply does not have the funds to buy the product.

The Talmud[1] states that raising the owner's expectation of making a sale, and then disappointing him causes pain and is a violation of onas devarim [harmful words].[iv""]

Everyone's time is valuable. We only have so many hours to work. In many companies, government organization, non-profits and other entities, every minute matters. In consulting, accounting and law firms, employees bill by the hour, if not every portions of an hour (e.g., fifteen minute increments). Every minute spent asking questions about one vendor could be time the vendor could spend selling to someone else.

In one famous men's clothing store, the customers know the product is good, and customers are expected to buy a product quickly. One would even say, if you don't know what you want, go home. While harsh, the overall point is that one must know if they will buy the item, and not waste valuable time of the seller.

Window shopping, simply quietly looking at the products from the outside, provides an excellent example of a workable workaround. If someone would not buy products at a store, but wants to admire the artwork, one can look from the outside; look at the colors and textures. A good general rule is not to go into the store unless one is eighty percent likely to buy a product. This is the right thing to do, as it doesn't waste valuable time of the store salespeople.

While Rabbis recommended not asking for prices (for products that people cannot afford) many years ago, the information is still relevant today. The importance of not asking a price can apply to other items. A recruiter might go onto LinkedIn or other websites, and identify candidates for positions at a company. It would not be appropriate for the candidate to call the recruiter to find out the information about the job, the salary, location,

---

[1] The Talmud is an encyclopedia-sized series of books that included voluminous number of rules and stories that Rabbis wrote millennia ago. It is a combination of two books, the Mishnah, completed around 200 CE (AD), and the Gemara, and was completed around 500 of the.

and other information if the candidate does not have an intention of applying for the job. Someone should not test drive a car that they can't afford. A professional should not interview for a position is the individual is not truly interested in the job. Someone should probably not contact realtors to look at houses for which one cannot obtain a mortgage.

2. Do Not Steal

One of the Ten Commandments simply states that "Ye shall not steal." (Leviticus 19:11[v]) It seems obvious that people should not steal from their own company, restaurants, grocery stores, or other commercial establishments.

Yet, consumers often steal clothing, food and other goods from stores. Stores have signs asking people not to shoplift, shoplifters will be persecuted, and that a camera will take videos. Shoplifting (as well as other employee theft) is a worldwide problem, and in costs companies over $112 billion in 2012[vi]. In addition, companies have to spend money just to avoid theft; companies spend $12 billion a year to try to avoid shoplifting.[vii]

Stealing means more than simple theft. Consumers should avoid buying items that could perpetuate more stealing (see Chapter 3). Parents should teach children to obtain employment so that children won't grow up and steal to survive (see Chapter 4). Parents of course should not steal. If a child sees a parent stealing packets of sugar from a restaurant, the children may get the idea that stealing is OK. In a related matter about stealing, a Rabbi noted that a child was going to a Jewish day school. The parent paid thousands of dollars to send the student to school, partly to get a great moral education. The parent stole goods from a store in front of the child. Though the goal of the school was to learn more about ethics, the act of stealing negated much of the knowledge the student learned. So it seems that the tuition was wasted.

Even stealing small office supplies, the pens and paper, is not valid. One Rabbi stated "when man robs his fellow even the value of a pertuah [an ancient coin worth almost nothing], it is though he had had his life taken away from him."[viii]

3. Do Not Buy Stolen Goods

While the basic rules for stealing seem obvious, the Rabbis developed other nuanced rules. A major device of the Rabbis is to build a wall around wall (create additional, more stringent rules) to help ensure people do not break the rule. For example, the Torah does not allow people to have sex before marriage. The Rabbis also made rules that prevented unrelated people in the opposite gender from even touching each other: "While the words "shomer negiah" literally mean "observant of touch", the term refers to someone who refrains from physical contact with members of the opposite sex. Originally known in texts simply as "negiah," the practice generally excludes one's immediate family members--a spouse, children, parents, siblings, and grandparents"[ix].

Another example of a wall around a wall is the rule to not buy stolen goods; beyond just not stealing, Rabbis stated that one should not buy items that are obviously stolen. One of the greatest Rabbis, Maimonides stated the following:

> "One may not buy from a thief the goods he has stolen, and to do so is a great transgression because it strengthens the hands of those who violate the law and causes the thief to continue to steal, for if the thief would find no buyer he would not steal…[x]"

The quote above, though written hundreds of years ago, still resonates today, as people continue to sadly sell stolen goods. Selling stolen goods remains prevalent. There is actually a slang term for selling the goods – "fencing". For example, the FBI convicted a fraudster that used people to steal over-the-counter medicine, baby products and other goods, then selling the products:

> " a multi-million-dollar, multi-state criminal enterprise where he received stolen over-the-counter (OTC) medicine, baby formula, health and beauty supplies, and shampoo for later re-packaging and shipping. This criminal enterprise, among other things, engaged in using "boosters," primarily undocumented Central Americans, to steal over-the-counter medication and baby formula. A booster is a criminal who steals goods and merchandise not for personal use but for re-sale to a "fence" for a fraction of its retail value. A fence is a person who receives stolen goods and merchandise from boosters and others. The fence then re-sells the stolen goods and merchandise to third parties for a profit." [xi]

Some criminals actually use the popular internet site Reddit to discuss methods to sell stolen goods. One post spewed the following:

> "I am trying to find a UK fencer (sell "obtained" goods on my behalf). Anyone have any recommendations or experiences with any vendors?" asks the original poster on the UK Fencing thread, who goes by the screen name of milkybarkid_ta."[xii]

American law correlates with rabbinic law. United States Code states that it is illegal to sell stolen goods. One who sells stolen goods will face a punishment:

> [Someone who] "receives, possesses, conceals, stores, barters, sells, or disposes of any goods, wares, or merchandise, securities, or money of the value of $5,000 or more, or pledges or accepts as security for a loan any goods, wares, or merchandise, or securities, of the value of $500 or more, which have crossed a State or United States boundary after being stolen, unlawfully converted, or taken, knowing the same to have been stolen, unlawfully converted, or taken"[xiii]

Another issue is people buying goods that are illicitly copied ("pirated"). In many places around the United States and the world, street vendors will sell obviously pirated movies, clothes, purses and other products. For example, a news show noted that some people would be happy to buy some purses that are obviously fake, but close to the genuine article. In the 1990s, Napster allowed people to download music for free. The Napster phenomenon shows how prevalent stealing can be. I early 2000s, the economy was growing, unemployment was low, and America was in an economic expansionary time at the end of the Cold War and before 9/11. Yet, many people simply downloaded music for free from the internet. Even large bands, such as Metallica, a famous "Heavy Metal" rock group, had issues. Metallica actually sued Napster – this upset many fans. In fact, an article stated that Metallica's lawsuit is another reason to "hate Metallica." One ex-fan stated that "I was once really into Metallica. But since the Napster thing, this and who knows what else. They are really getting bad.."[xiv]

Piracy remains an enormous problem. For example, a computer magazine published an article about the 10 most pirated movies. Effectively, so many people stole movies online that a magazine actually listed the top ten stolen movies. [xv]

Not only do Rabbis state that one should not buy stolen goods, but even that one does a good deed (mitzvah) using stolen goods, the good deed simply does not "count". For example, one cannot use a stolen myrtle branch to perform a ritual mitzvah, as listed in Sukkah 3:1 in the Mishnah[xvi]. Note that a lulav is a mix of three types of plants, and is used to perform a ritual deed during the Jewish holiday of Sukkot

B. Employee Responsibilities

The vast majority of people will, at some point, be employees. A career is a multi-decade journey. The journey begins years before the employee starts working; the journey commences with a child's education – at home and in the classroom. Some high school students work while in school, while tens of millions will start full-time employment after high school, undergraduate, or graduate school. The Bible and the Rabbis that interpreted the Bible provide many guidelines for employees.

4. Providing a Skill

Judaism contains important rules about teaching children. For example, one of the most important prayers in Judaism (the Shema, which means "listen") states that "And ye shall teach them your children, speaking of them when thou sittest in thine house, and when thou walkest by the way, when thou liest down, and when thou risest up." [xvii]

In addition to teaching children important rules about prayers, dietary restrictions (kashrut), and other matters, Rabbis also taught the importance about learning a craft: "The ancient rabbis put great value on having a skill or trade on which people could depend for their livelihood."[xviii] The following quote shows the emphasis Rabbis put on the developing skill, in the Babylonian Talmud, chapter Kiddushin 30b, versus 31:

> "'R. Judah said: He who does not teach him a craft teaches him brigandage. "Brigandage"! can you think so? — But it is like teaching him brigandage'. Wherein do they differ? — They differ where he teaches him business." [xix]

This is valuable advice. Basically, the Rabbis stated that if someone does not teach their child skills needed to gain employment, it as if the person is teaching the child to steal. It is imperative to teach one's children about work and careers. My father emphasized the importance of getting a job, and said that accounting is a great field. I liked accounting in college and majored in Commerce (concentration in accounting). The field of accounting has provided me steady income and consistent employment since I graduated college in 1999, despite two recessions.

In turn, I hope to also motivate my newborn son to obtain the skills and have the proper work ethic needed to obtain and maintain employment. I'm hopeful that I can steer my son in a good career path, so that he can also be employed year after year. I hope that he can stand on his two feet economically, and if he decides to marry and have children, also support his family. Following are some pictures of my son. While I realize it may be year until my son starts working, I'm still cognizant of the importance of teaching him the lessons needed put him into the right course in his career, as well as teaching him proper ethical values I hope he will use in his career.

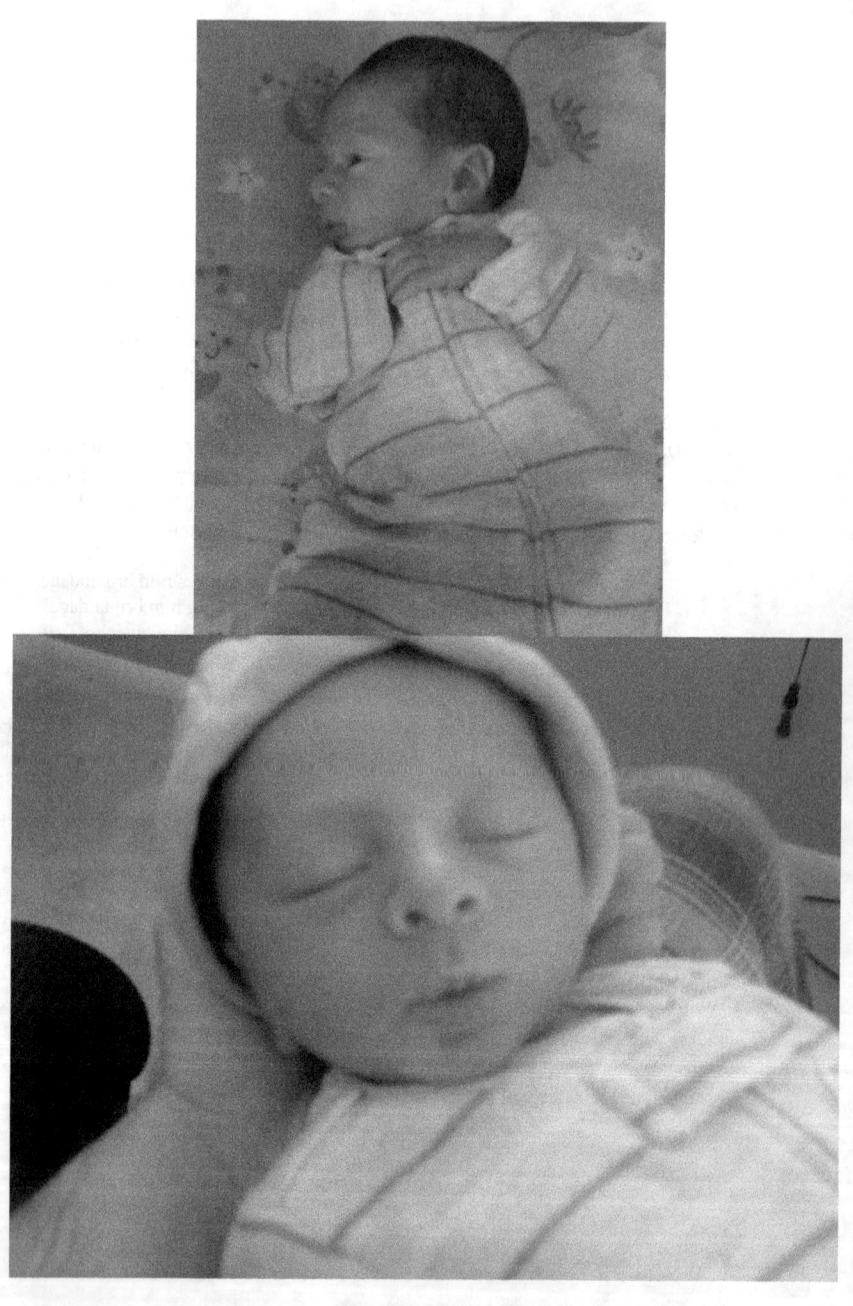

In addition to parents teaching their children about careers, in today's day and age, others can also provide some valuable insight – teachers, coaches, siblings, grandparents, etc. For example, many wrestling coaches take an active interest in their wrestlers – not just on the wrestling mat, but in the classroom and in their career.[2] One coach spoke with some wrestlers, and knew the wrestlers' work ethic and preferences. For example, the coach recommended that a wrestler go into the Marine Corps (the Marines). The wrestler joined the Marines, persevered through a challenging boot camp (the discipline and work ethic from high school wrestling was very helpful to grapple with the rigors of Marine boot camp), and proudly returned to practice during a break from the Marines. The wrestler also invited some coaches to a party to celebrate the former wrestler joining the Marines and finishing boot camp, in some ways likely as a thank-you.

Maimonides provides other very helpful guidance; he lists several forms of charity, with the highest form is that one should help one help themselves. In this way, helping to provide a skill is therefore truly the highest form of charity – not giving money, but helping people obtain a career.

The importance of teaching a valuable skill cannot be underestimated. In 2012, only half of college graduates (graduating since 2006) had a full-time position. The situation is even worse for students graduating after 2009: Fewer than half of college graduates found their first job within 12 months of graduating ."[xx] The situation is so dire that some students, in fact take full-time unpaid internships.[xxi]

The importance of teaching children (as well as students and siblings) about career fields can help not only one's family, but the overall economy. There is a mismatch of skills to job opportunities, as job-seekers do not meet the needs of employers. If students go into fields that are growing, it will help better match the short-term and long-term needs. Simply put, students should be encouraged to go into fields that are hiring (or long-term will hire). The legendary strategic consulting firm McKinsey & Company stated that there is a need to develop employee skills to meet the employer needs[xxii]. In the aggregate, providing a more focused work force will put more people into jobs, and provide employers with more qualified employees.

---

[2] For more information about wrestling, and the influence of wrestling coaches, a good resource is Lessons from the Wrestling Mat - Life lessons from a quarter century of coaching and competing (https://www.amazon.com/Lessons-Wrestling-Mat-coaching-competing-ebook/dp/B01F0QFFXA?ie=UTF8&keywords=lessons%20from%20the%20wrestling%20mat&qid=1463363983&ref_=sr_1_1&s=books&sr=1-1).

5. Importance to Find Dignity in All Work

Another important concept is the inherent dignity of all work. All work matters, from the teachers in the classroom to the cashier in Costco. For example, Talmud Chapter Berakhot 8a notes the following: "One who earns by the efforts of his own hands stands even higher than one who is completely God-fearing". The Rabbis who wrote the Talmud had differing viewpoints about working, though many stated that all work matters. One story in the Talmud states the following: "When R. Judah went to the Beth ha-Midrash…he used to take a pitcher on his shoulders [to sit on], saying. 'Great is labour, for it honours the worker.'…R. Simeon used to carry a basket upon his shoulders, saying likewise, 'Great is labour, for it honors the worker.'"xxiii

Following is another section from the Talmud, as well as more recent Rabbi's interpretation:

> Rabbi Joshua ben Levi said: When the Holy and Blessed One told Adam, "Thorns and thistles shall it sprout for you, but your food shall be the grasses of the field," Adam began to well up with tears. "Master of the Universe, shall my ass and I both eat at the same trough??" But as soon as God said to him [immediately following] "By the sweat of your brow shall you get bread to eat," his spirits were soothed. Grasses of the field: raw, natural, unprocessed food. What animals eat…..But as soon as God said to him, in the very next verse, "by the sweat of your brow shall you get bread to eat," his spirits were soothed. This idea that we take, again, the average person and say "tell me what the pshat / contextual meaning is here," that this is a continuation of a curse, it's only by the sweat of your brow that you'll get any bread -- it's flipped over in this text to become kind of a [consolation] for what's come before. If you are willing to put in some elbow grease, you'll have bread. And Adam is happy with that. If he gets to work he'll see the fruits of his labor. This is an element of dignity.xxiv

One issue is the counterproductive concept that only certain jobs (e.g., office jobs) are appropriate for college-educated people. Some think that people who went to college should only work in an office, and should not have to use their hands. This creates glut of people in certain fields (e.g., law), and a lack of enough people in other fields. The law market is flooded, and some lawyers are unable to find jobs in their field, despite four years of undergraduate study, three years of law school, and thousands of dollars in debt. Yet, other jobs remain unfilled, jobs that require hard physical labor in the fields. The employers will sometimes not find enough people to work.

Even within the "white-collar" realm, often the employees don't want to do the tacit, "grunt" work. In a consulting company, many applicants desired to be a project manager, as opposed to a project worker. Many professionals want to look at a chart that shows the status of work completed, assign others to do work (e.g., analysis, testing, coding, etc.) instead of actually doing the tacit work. Schools frequently exacerbate the issues. For example; even in the information technology field, several professors at a graduate program gave the impression to students that the students would be managing technology, instead of analyzing, working and producing technology. This can create issues later, for example, as employees do not learn the actual tacit work. For example, one employee received several degrees in business from highly-ranked institutions. The employee was taught about the people that founded and managed the FedEx Corporation. The employee was very upset when the employee had to make FedEx envelopes at work - instead of running and founding FedEx, the employee stuffed FedEx envelopes.

The Rabbis note that all work is important, that working with one's hands or one's mind is important is still sage advice. The US economy, as well as a worldwide economy, has had many issues with unemployment and underemployment. Yet there are millions of unfilled positions. Therefore, it would be very helpful for more people to take more tacit jobs.

6. Though Shalt Have an Accurate Resume

One of the first steps in an employee's career is creating the resume. Almost all employees will search for another job at some point/time in their career (people rarely get one job after undergraduate/graduate school/high school, and keep the job their entire life). Most employers will require that applicants provide a resume.

The Rabbis cautioned against providing "false impressions", which the Rabbis called "undeserved goodwill", meaning that people will incorrectly "attribute to you something …. which you fail to correct." The Rabbis cautioned against giving a façade of kindness that was not accurate. For example, the Rabbis stated that one should not give the impression to guests that a container of wine will be used only for the guest (this denotes respect, as it shows the host is only going to use wine for the guest), the host will actually sell the wine to someone else.[xxv]

While being honest on a resume might seem obvious, many people lie on resumes. For example, numerous high-profile candidates have lied on their resumes. A basketball coach offered a multi-million dollar contract to coach college basketball lied – and ultimately lost a $5 million contract.[xxvi] One of the most infamous situations was George O'Leary, who lost one of the most coveted jobs in college football – head coach of the storied Notre Dame team. A man lost a position as CEO of Radio Shack for lying on his resume. In 2014, a Vice President of Wal-Mart lost his job because he lied about getting a college degree.[xxvii]

These lies in the resumes are, unfortunately, not just anecdotal examples from high-profile celebrities. Nearly half of job-seekers lie on their resumes:

> "The tendency to embellish information on a resume is so widespread, nearly half (46 percent) of job applicants commit some form of resume fraud, according to ADP, the human capital management and research firm."[xxviii]

Lying on one's resume can lead to numerous issues. In addition to being fired from a positon, there are long-term issues even if the employer does not learn about the lie. If too many people lie about having technical skills to get jobs, companies might erroneously think that the companies can easily find people with certain technical skills. This creates a situation in which people might have a motivation to lie to get a job. Another problem is that the employee may state they have certain skills, then fail at their job, as they lack certain skills. This creates problems for the employee and the employer: the employer has the challenge of training an employee, or firing them. The lying employees will effectively truly only punish themselves. The employee may have very long hours to properly do work, and go through the stress of struggling in a job. At a consulting firm, people are placed into different positions via resumes. So if people lie about their abilities, the people will be incorrectly placed into positions where they can't meet the requirements. The employees may struggle, and the clients would get employees that lack the requisite skills.

7. The Good Deed of Loaning Money

The Rabbis recommend loaning money. Loaning money was not just an economic transaction, or a way to generate interest, but actually a mitzvah (righteous act). It is a good deed to loan to the poor. The Torah states (in Deuteronomy 15:7-8):

> If there be among you a poor man of one of thy brethren within any of thy gates in thy land which the LORD thy God giveth thee, thou shalt not harden thine heart, nor shut thine hand from thy poor brother:

> but thou shalt open thine hand wide unto him, and shalt surely lend him sufficient for his need, in that which he wanteth

Jewish law states that one should loan money, as well as objects. At the same point, Jewish law is reasonable - one should not loan to those who are not likely to repay the loan. [xxix] For example, if Bob Smith (not a real person) has a record of not repaying a lender, the lender would not be obligated to loan money to Bob.

Another important caveat is that someone should only make a loan if the loaner is "capable". The lender should not go into financial distress due to the loan. This is similar for giving charity; Judaism teaches not to give so much that one become poor: "charity is an obligation, but there are limits. To give away all of your possessions and make yourself poor is prohibited."[xxx] As the above statement shows, lending to the poor is a good deed. Directly loaning is actually more important than donating money to charity.

The Rabbis wisely note the intensity of the loaner's response. The creditor decides to specifically contact someone for a loan, which can be difficult for most people. Hence, the Rabbis realize the desperation of the creditor. At the same point, the creditor has an obligation to repay the loan. The creditor should also try to save their money, and should strive not to take on debt. For example, someone who borrows money to get one's significant other out of jail shouldn't be frequently partying, watching concerts, and partaking in other entertainment options while the loan remains unpaid.

Loaning to a business

The Rabbis also recommend loaning to help businesses. The Talmud states "He who lends money is greater than he who performs charity, and he who forms a partnership is greater than all." The concept is that by loaning to businesses, such as partnerships, the lenders can provide needed funds to help grow businesses. The business receiving the loan would then be able to grow and hire more people, which should help the community. The goal is a business is to help the community, according to the Talmud. [xxxi]

Maimonides had an important hierarchy of the types of charity – his listing included eight categories. The lowest is giving grudgingly (e.g., to "aggressive panhandling"), while the second lowest is giving less than a requested amount (e.g., a charitable organization asked for $100, and the person gives $50). The highest form of charity is helping someone help themselves. This is "providing assistance by helping people find work, offering a loan, or entering into a partnership, in order to help start or maintain the business."[xxxii]

Just as Rabbis recommended loaning funds many years ago, today many groups recommend loaning small amounts of money to help start or grow small businesses (microfinance). Microfinance was started by a bank that the 2006 Nobel Peace Prize winner Muhammad Yunus founded. Mr. Yunus actually started by loaning his own money to villagers in Bangladesh. He tried to get banks to loan to the villagers, and the banks refused. So he actually borrowed money himself, then loaned to the villagers. The villagers consistently repaid the loans, and eventually Mr. Yunus started a bank[xxxiii]. While microfinance began in Bangladesh, microfinance has spread to other nations. Since the USA financial crises in the late 2000s (also known as the Great Recession), many US creditors have used microfinance, including those fledging businesses that would be unable to get loans or credit cards. In fact, a microfinance group in the USA has loaned over $100 million to help various small businesses. [xxxiv]

Another example is the Whole Foods Foundation (the "Foundation"), owned by the grocery store Whole Foods. The Foundation provides modest (less than two hundred dollars) loans to people in the developing world. The loans require no collateral or credit history (this is more similar to loans that Rabbis recommend, and different from banks). The loans have been both widespread and successful: "the Foundation has witnessed a payback rate of 97 percent on the staggering $32,095,574 (U.S.) committed to some 224,772 microcredit clients in 54 countries globally. Indeed, entire families and communities are buoyed each time an enterprising but capital-poor woman is able to bring goods or services to market; the Foundation estimates a total of 1,342,275 souls have been supported through the above-mentioned 224,772 microcredit clients." [xxxv] A Whole Foods store in Washington, DC provides a fascinating map that shows that many nations that benefit from the American company.

8. Spending Wisely – Though shalt not Go into debt

Thousands of years before the debt crises in the late 2000s, the Talmud strongly recommended that people avoid debt. The Talmud stated that it is better to eat poorly and have no debt than to eat well and have debt. The Talmud stated that one should "eat vegetables and fear no creditors rather than eat duck and hide." This statement basically means that individuals and companies should avoid taking on too much debt, creating further problems – "it calls on companies and individuals not to spend beyond their means. Once in debt, you are always fearful of creditors and the humiliation that being in debt can bring." [xxxvi] Note the nuance of the Rabbis' logic – while it is a good deed to loan money, ultimately, people should try to avoid getting into the situation in which they will need to borrow.

In the business world, however, debt is much different. One of the tenants of finance is the importance of making as much money as possible using the least amount of equity (assets a company owes less debt). The concept is leverage – loaning from others, and making money from the loaned money. For example, a company could loan $1 billion from a bank, pay 6 percent interest, and make 10 percent on investments. Someone could buy a house with $40,000 down, buy house for $200,000, then sell house, and the house would increase in value to $250,000. The person could then sell, making a $50,000 profit (less closing costs). This could result in making a huge amount of money. In fact, some students in business school courses gave presentations encouraging companies to increase debt.

Debt has a down side. For example, if a house with a mortgage decreases in value, one would actually owe more on the house than equity – so-called upside down mortgage. For example, one woman thought she would make money on a second home. She put a small amount down on the house, took on hundreds of thousands of debt, expecting the price to increase on the house. The price, however, decreased during the housing bust of the late 2000s. She owed the mortgage, and simply could not pay the monthly fees – and could not sell the home. This created a huge financial problem. Many people worldwide have the same issues.

The refusal to pay down debt can destroy also relationships. In one church, a man asked for a loan. He loaned money to another congregate. The debtor would see the man every day, never mentioning the loan. The loaner became disgusted and disappointed with the congregate. He confided to a friend about the debtor [let's call the debtor Mr. Smith] – "everyone I see Mr. Smith, all I can see is the hundreds he owes me. It doesn't matter what the debtor says about religion, the bible, or family. He's the guy that owes me money."

In fact, debt collection remains a strong industry in the United States. Many companies make money simply collecting debt. Parts of federal agencies focus on collecting debt. Many people in corporations, not for profits, and government entities spent countless hours tracking debt. The situation is stressful for the debtors. There are people who will not answer a phone call, for fear the person calling may be a creditor.

Not paying back bills can cause huge problems. A candidate attempted to obtain high-paying job at an outstanding organization. The job paid over $120,000 a year, with excellent benefits and work-life balance. The person applying (the candidate) was given a job offer, after beating numerous well-qualified competitors. The candidate, however, had several debts. The candidate's debts were so bad that the candidate did not obtain a security clearance[3]. As the candidate was unable to obtain a clearance, the employer rescinded the job offer. This situation caused not only the employee disappointment, but also resulted in problems for the potential employer. The employer interviewed many people for the position, and wound up wasting time and resources in interviewing a candidate who could not work in the position. There might have been other candidates who did not get the job, and may have found other opportunities in the mean-time (while someone else was selected). Many people were inconvenienced in this situation. This is not, unfortunately, an anomaly. This situation happened sometimes, showing the issues that occur when people don't pay their bills. [4]

Not only can debt destroy the chances of getting a job, but debt can even lead to an employee losing a job. Another employee received a job opportunity, after struggling to get a new position for several years. The job opportunity paid well and was in his field of knowledge. He was hired for the job, yet the organization learned (after he started working) that he had outstanding debt. The employer decided the debt was too large, and decided to fire him. He spent years looking for another position and almost become homeless.

Another salient example of debt is Virginia ex-Governor. He took on enormous debt when he purchased a second home, and probably expected to make a profit on the home. He was unable to pay a mortgage of $12,000 a month. He allegedly then started getting

---

[3] Employees must have relatively limited debt in order to keep a security clearance, a requirement for many jobs. One idea is that if someone had too much debt, the person may sell value secrets to a nation's enemies.

[4] I hope to also teach me son to pay his debts, to be responsible. This could help him immensely.

questionable loans from others. One might strongly consider that the debt was a major problem that may have led to taking improper loans. For more information about the situation, see chapter 34.

9. Do Not Steal Company Time

In the first book of the Bible (Genesis), Jacob wanted to marry Rachel. Jacob's father in law, Laban, stated that Jacob would have to work for seven years in order to marry Rachel. Laban, tricked Jacob, and on the wedding day, when Jacob opened the veil, it was actually Leah (Rachel's sister) that Jacob married. Jacob was tricked into marrying the wrong women; Jacob actually had to work seven years for Leah, and then another seven years for Rachel.[5] Jacob could have been bitter and worked little, putting in minimum effort to let the long time pass easily. Jacob, however, worked very hard. A very important scholar, Moses Ben (son of) Maimon (RaMBaM; usually called Maimonides) writes the following:

> just as an employer may not withhold the wages of his workers, so too the worker may not steal time from his work. … and he is obligated to work with all of his strength, as Yaakov HaTzaddick [Jacob] declared, "for I have worked for your father [Laven] with all of my strength.' The Ranbam deduces the responsibilities of an employer from the relationship between Yaakov [Jacob] and Laban…. One would think that when dealing with such an evil person ("Lavan]…a person would be entitled to "fight fire with fire" and resort to trickery to protect himself. Yet, Yaakov described his years of labor for Lavan as follows: … "by day, heat consumed me, and snow by night; my sleep drifted before my eyes…" Yaakov refused to lower his standards, and refused to compromise his personal integrity, even under such trying circumstances. This truly should be our model on which our sense of honesty and obligation to our employers should be based.[xxxvii]

In today's business world, the ability to do non-work related activities on the job has multiplied. The business world is full of endless distractions during the work day – everything from holiday shopping, Facebook, Twitter, and personal email. With the enhanced use of mobile phones, the number of distractions has exploded. Some employers, due to cyber-security concerns, disallow employees from using streamlining audio or email. Other companies have fewer rules, and instead opt for general guidance to limit usage of email.

Having another job can also be a disruptive distraction. Companies sometimes have rules that try to avoid employees having other jobs. For example, some large accounting /

---

[5] In Jewish weddings, there is a part of the ceremony in which the groom helps ensure that he is marrying the right person; this harks back to the story of Jacob marrying Leah instead of Rachel.

consulting firms have limitations for a second job. Some entities might require signing a form to disallow a second job.

It is important not to steal company time. In addition to the ethical issues, stealing time could cause problems. A manager could complain to an employee that spends too much time on the internet; some managers were very upset at employees that squandered too much time online, even documenting complaints in a review. This is a situation in which following rules that are millennia old can still help one in their current job and future career opportunities.

10. Confidentiality – Keeping a Secret a Secret – Personal

Year ago, Rabbis noted the importance of confidentiality, taking a story from the Torah as a proof text:

> *Rabba stated: From where do we learn that if one relates something to another, the receiver of this information is prohibited from repeating it to others without permission to do so? As it is written (Leviticus 1:1): "And the Lord spoke to him in the Tent of Meeting, to say." - Babylonian Talmud; Tractate Yoma P 4 Col 2*[xxxviii]

In the business world, confidentiality is extremely important. For example, an employee working for a technology company may need to sign an agreement to not disclose secrets, including about proprietary technological items. In other entities, it is extremely important to keep secrets, such as items dealing with national security, company contracts, bids on jobs, and the job search.

In a non-profit organization, an accountant (let's call her "Jill") experienced a lack of confidentiality. A consultant to a company confided to Jill, telling Jill that he (the consultant) was leaving the consulting firm for whom he worked. The consultant asked Jill not to tell others, and Jill promised. Other consultants also worked on the project. Despite the promise of confidentiality, Jill told the consultant's manager. This created stress for the employee. The auditor would probably never trust Jill, and probably not help her in the future. The auditor's manager lost respect for the consultant, and did not provide help to the consultant in future years.

Following is another example of lack confidentiality. An employee goes to a company's Ombudsman. The Ombudsman's job was to listen to the employee's issues, provide advice, and keep strict confidentiality. In one employer, the Ombudsman recorded information from an employee requesting help, and immediately the Ombudsman informed senior management about the issue, even naming specific employee that had the complaint. The employee was very upset, and others in the entity found out about the Ombudsman.

Edward Snowden was a government contractor. He leaked secretive data from the National Security Agency. He claimed to have obtained ""internet history, emails, text messages, calls and passwords." The information that Snowden provided may likely have had tragic consequences. Lord West, a former Admiral and government official from the UK stated: "Edward Snowden leaks cost lives, say experts as extremists 'changed their tactics'."[xxxix]

11. L'shan Hora – Gossiping at Work – Responsibility to Maintain One's Good Name

Another violation in the Torah is malicious gossip. Miriam, Moses' sister, complained about Moses because he married Ethiopian woman. G-d was very upset at Miriam's gossip, and punished Miriam by inflicting her with a skin disease (Numbers 12:1-10). Miriam was outcaste from Israel for a few days her saying rude things about Moses behind his back. In business, as an employee, manager, or peers have an obligation to not talk ill of coworkers.

The Rabbis were also opposed to gossip, as rumors can destroy one's reputation. A rabbi said "A person's tongue is more powerful than his sword. A sword can only kill someone who is nearby; a tongue can cause the death of someone who is far away." The Rabbis created a very complex series of rules against gossip. [xl] The Chofetz Chaim, a very important Rabbi focused on the sin of loshon hora (evil language/pernicious gossip). He wrote extensionally on ways to avoid loshon hora.

Today, an employee can do more than just spread malicious gossip by conversation in person or via the phone. Employees can spread gossip to thousands, if not millions, via the internet. In one situation, an employee was fired due to a negative post on Facebook – "A company that fired a worker after she posted negative remarks about her boss on Facebook". The employee ultimately was able to settle the situation, after the employee worked through the employee's union and filed against the employer, via the National Labor Relations Board[xli].

Unfortunately, human nature has probably not changed, but technology has. Moses didn't have the use of a cell phone, internet, or Twitter. People are upset at their neighbors, coworkers, bosses, etc. And the internet provides an easy way to criticize others – without even seeing any other person. It is frankly easy and cowardly to write an email, Facebook post, or Twitter post criticizing someone else. Writing an email, posting on Facebook or via Twitter can take seconds. But the damage can be nearly permanent.

Gossiping can hurt behind one's back:

> At one company, two employees complained about their manager, but didn't tell the manager the complaints. There was no opportunity for the employee to retort the criticism, or improve, to change, to go back on the right path.
>
> From a practical standpoint, stating negative items behind one's back can result in other issues. If a person speak[s] ill about one person, then the

person hearing the conversation might think that the person might speak ill of him or her! In this case, the gossip-manger may hurt his/her chances

One form of malicious gossip (lashon hora) is critical words. Harvard teaches the importance of not criticizing in front of others. It's a well-known in management not to criticize in front of other coworkers. In general, this is a bad idea. For some workers it can be a bigger issue, especially in certain cultures:

> One of their greatest fears of first generation Hispanics, is that their supervisor will attempt to discipline them on the spot in front of his or her coworkers. While the supervisor may feel that this method of discipline may be the most effective way to prevent future mistakes, the employee feels humiliated and embarrassed at being singled out. [xlii]

At one entity, an employee (let's call the employee Pat) was upset at Joe --- wrote an email criticizing Joe's work product. Pat wrote the email to Joe's boss, causing issues for Joe. Joe saw the email, and was upset at Pat, ruining any hope of a career relationship.

Slandering a boss or colleague on Twitter is not only unethical, but it is also could be career detriment. One site states: "What happens when you go to apply for another job and it's discovered (and it will be) that you've trash-talked your last supervisor on Facebook or Twitter?... "Oh, goody," thinks the hiring manager, "let's hire this person who is immature and impulsive and unprofessional enough to call her last boss a 'big fat dummy head.' Can't wait to see what she says about us if she has a bad day."[xliii]

At another employer, an employee was posting harshly negative remarks about the employee's manager on Facebook the employees friends saw the posting, and eventually the manager was rumored to call the police. The employee's own mother saw the posting, and was very upset.

Of course, there are limits. What if you had a friend applying for a position at company XYZ, where you work? The friend would like to work at a place with job security and work/life balance. Your company fires many employees, and works employees many hours. Should you tell your friend about the issues?

Another major issue is when the media (e.g., magazines or newspapers) makes pernicious and harmful accusations against people and organizations. The words have caused damage. The media has been full of articles that accuse people of numerous crimes, such as child abuse. Some of these accusations are sadly true. Yet, others are unfounded and can cause significant damage to innocent people, teams, and organizations. Many articles have resulted in putting organizations and people in a horrible and negative light, led to people losing their jobs, caused tremendous embarrassment and shame, and caused vandalism. Some groups have fought back and sued the writers that spewed such hateful and malicious words, but the damage was already done. Authors have fabricated or stories or assumed people were guilty – though the people and/or organizations were proven innocent, including in court. Journalists today can learn from the Rabbis' words centuries ago about what not to say. Or write. Or email. Or tweet. Or post in Facebook.

12. Taking a Sabbath (or other) Break - Employee Responsibilities

One company was merging with another large company. The head of the company said that he would do everything in his power to ensure the merger was successful. The head of the company worked very hard on the merger, putting all his efforts into the merger. By the time the merger was finished, so was his marriage – he divorced his wife during the merger, likely due to stress of the merger. An executive (a partner) at the large accounting firm was pleased that he was able to watch a grand total of one swimming meet for his daughter during the year, as opposed to years in which the partner saw no swimming meets.

The work place is probably littered with stories of executives, manager, and employees who have worked so hard for so long that their personal lives suffer. Or perhaps there personal lives have ceased to exist. It is important to take a break from work.

In the Torah, the idea is that the Shabbas, from sunset Friday night to sunset Saturday night, should be a break from work. While not everyone has religious beliefs to take a break on Shabbos, the concept of taking a break is very important. Many employees will quit their jobs, or decide to not go into certain management paths, because they simply get no break. The employees are too tired to keep the long hours, leaving their job before the employees got major promotions. For example, one employee quit the corporate world and a chance and getting a major promotion and a huge salary, because he was so tired of working for so long – a break would have helped him. Taking a break can help employees stay longer in jobs, and eventually reach new heights in their careers.

C.   Employer Responsibilities

In a business world, the emphasis is often on the bottom line. This often means cutting the budget as much as possible and increasing revenue. Currently, businesses (and government agencies, as well as non-profits) focus on doing more with less. Businesses will avoid taking actions that will cause the company to get more revenue, or stakeholders will be unwilling to pay more money for products or services.

While providing profit is an important goal, so is taking care of all employees. This includes the moment that the employers start to recruit potential employees, the point at which employees enter the work place ("on-boarding"), throughout employment, and even after the employees leaves the company – either due to the employee leaving on his/her own, or the employer deciding to fire the employee (see chart later below).

Employee Life Cycle

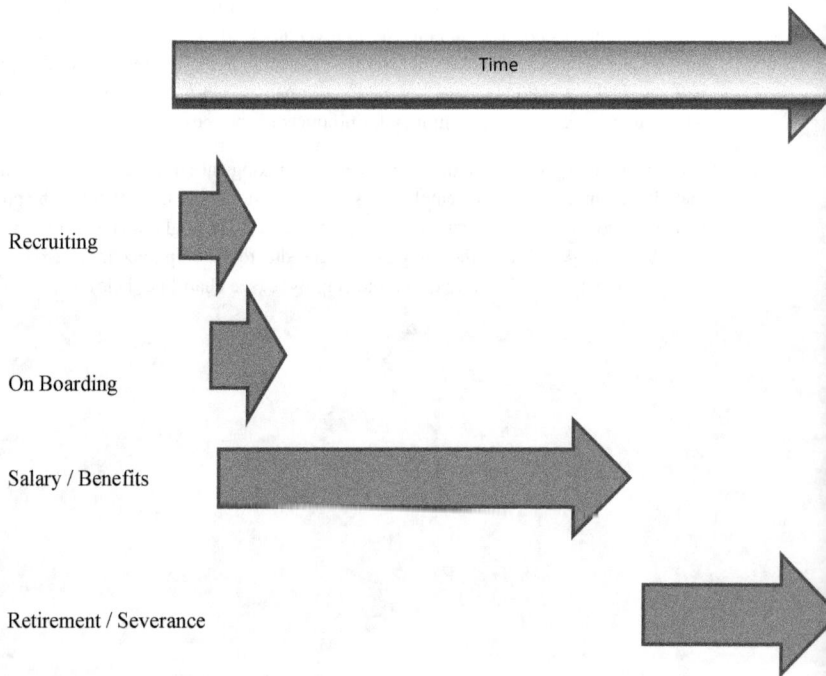

Recruiting

On Boarding

Salary / Benefits

Retirement / Severance

13. Don't Do What is Hateful to Others

Years before the golden rule ("Love they neighbor as thyself"), an important Rabbi had a similar rule. In a very famous story, a gentile asked Rabbi Hillel to explain the Torah while standing on one foot. Rabbi Hillel stated "whatever is hateful onto thee, do it not to thy fellow man. That is the whole of Torah. The rest is commentary." [xliv]

From this advice, a manager should learn to simply not to take actions against their subordinates that would upset the manager, if the manager was on the other side of the action. Many managers fail in this aspect. For example, one senior manager at a large employer took weeks to approve travel vouchers (he just needed to review receipts and click one button to approve). The manager took weeks to make the simple approval. Yet, when the manager went on travel, the manager made numerous calls for someone to approve his travel – within days. Many of the rules in the next few pages have similar type guidance. Additionally, an employer's policies should use the guidance of not doing what is upsetting to him/herself.

14. Though Shalt Provide a Valid Job Offer

The employer/employee relationship truly begins when the employer provides the employee with a job offer, and the employee accepts. At that point, there is a valid contract. The employer is responsible for any loss the employee suffers if the employee loses other opportunities. [xlv] Therefore, if an employee were to rescind the job offer, the employer would owe the employee money, including losses.

This is a situation in which rabbinical rules and secular society statutes diverge. The rules in the USA are different than Jewish Law (Halachah). There are mixed rules in the market-place about damages for rescinding job offers:

> "in some states the "at-will" doctrine will bar the employee from recovering damages, but in some states the prospective employee can recover damages under the theory of "**promissory estoppel**" [a way to enforce a promise made to one person by another, or put another way, it's a way for the law to stop someone from denying that he or she made a promise] or "**detrimental reliance**.""[xlvi]

This topic is relevant in the modern day. During times of economic challenges, companies actually rescinded job offers or extended the start date. For example, in 2014, one large ("Big Law") firm actually rescinded the job offers for half of the new hires (associates). [xlvii]

15. Properly Entering the Workplace

It is important to properly help new employees in a new job. There are multiple challenges that new employees face, from learning about the business processes in the organization, administrative matters (e.g., requesting time for vacation/sick), nebulous unwritten rules, etc. New employees come from a variety of circumstances. It is best to "Ensure that new employees understand their role and how it relates to the rest of the workforce". [xlviii]

Many companies provide a mentor for new employees, which can be helpful. One company paired all new employees with a mentor from the day that the employees entered the company. Another large accounting firm even paired interns with a mentor to provide advice. In one firm, the mentor and the employee stayed in touch for decades after the employee left the company. In other entities, mentor and mentees are matched, and the relationship lasts for nine months.

Another method that companies use for new employees is putting new employees close to the customer. Some companies will start employees at a technical help desk, to expose employees to the end customer. The company FreshBooks, for example, has new employees work a month in the customer service department. This experience helps show employees "….a different kind of worldview around what service can be for customers." [xlix]

From an employee responsibility, beyond the basic formalities of providing an introduction to the workplace and a manager to introduce the new employees, there is more employers can and should do. For example, employers can have informal sessions for new employees, where the employees can learn about the unwritten rules about the company – the things that one should and should not do. This can be very helpful. Other companies have "high-level executives make contact with each employee during the interview of onboarding process." [l] This can also be helpful, in helping the employees better understand the company from a high level perspective.

16. Provide Proper Training

Teaching is extremely important in the Jewish tradition – this includes parents teaching children, Rabbis teaching congregations, and Rabbis teaching other Rabbis. The Talmudic chapter Bava Batra 21b states that "when you punish a pupil, only hit him with a shoe lace." Teachers should be "slow to anger" and the Talmud stresses that "learning should be enjoyable." In fact, some schools would put honey between pages to show that learning is sweet[6]. In the corporate world, sometimes instructors give candy to employees during training sessions. Also, it is important to be patient, and companies should realize that "students who don't learn as quickly or as thoroughly as others should not be penalized."[li]

Employers sometimes do not act in the methods that the Rabbis recommended in regards to corporate training. One manager thought that employees who attend training should be able to instantly learn and use information from training, and would be very upset if the employees did not instantly apply lessons. Yet, learning takes time, and managers should be patient.

Additionally, training is a very important and valuable benefit for an employee. The training itself should be more than just another tool to get employees to learn new skills. Employers should also consider training as a benefit – employees are often simply pleased to receive training. Many business journals write numerous articles about the "war for talent." Employers need employees with sought-after technical skills (e.g., people who have knowledge of mobile coding skills), and employers need to take steps to attract, keep and engage employees. As employees want training, it behooves employers to provide training opportunities. Providing these opportunities will likely make employees happier in their current jobs, and help attract talent. Many companies continue to struggle to keep top talent, and providing training is an excellent method to keep the top employees.

---

[6] To emulate this tradition, I actually provide candy to CPA review students, to make 3-4 hour classes more palatable.

17. Charity – Gift of Time

In addition to providing financial support, companies should also provide the gift of time. This gift is valuable – "one who gives a*prutah* (a small coin) to a poor person is blessed with six blessings but one who consoles a poor person is blessed with eleven blessings. (Baba Batra 9b)". [lii]

Many companies provide time (during the work day) for employees to perform community service. For example, certain employers may have interns do community service, while other times, it may be a concerted effort in which all employees participate. In some cases, a company may facilitate community service by coordinating events. For example, one large employer helped to work with a local organization to provide tutoring to junior high students. The employees tutored students in the evening, after work. Another company provided mentoring and tutoring at a local elementary school, and managers accommodated this by allowing employees to arrive late to work (e.g., 10 a.m.). A large consultancy, Accenture, actually gives some employees three days to work on charity projects.[liii]

Whether employees perform charity efforts to help themselves (e.g., resume builder) or to help others, the charity efforts can be very beneficial. The Rabbis smartly surmise that the "ulterior motive should not be a concern. Whether a person or company gives charity or self-serving reasons or for more righteous reasons, the recipient is still blessed by the act and the recipient still reaps the benefits." [liv]

Companies can not only provide time (or flexibility) for community service while employees are working for the employer, but also during breaks in one's career. For example, during the recessions in the early 2000s, the technology company Cisco downsized six thousand employees. Cisco offered employees the opportunity to still get some important benefits while helping the community – Cisco paid one-third of the employee's salaries if the employees worked for a non-profit entity in the community. Additionally, Cisco would provide stock options. Cisco also noted that the employees would be the "first to be rehired when the economy improved." [lv] This is an excellent example of helping the community and providing a method for employees to remain active when their simply are not enough positions.

18. Promptly Paying Employees and Vendors

The Bible states that workers should be paid within a reasonable period of time; the following passage is included with other sections that contain various important rules about treating employees. Deuteronomy 24:14-15 states:

> Thou shalt not oppress a hired servant that is poor and needy, whether he be of thy brethren, or of thy strangers that are in thy land within thy gates: at his day thou shalt give him his hire, neither shall the sun go down upon it; for he is poor, and setteth his heart upon it: lest he cry against thee unto the LORD, and it be sin unto thee.

The basic principle is that the consumer must pay the worker as soon as possible – the very same day that the employee worked. As with many rules from the Bible, Rabbis interpreted the rules to provide more guidance. Rabbis provide more guidance because sometimes the Bible provides fairly few words. The Rabbis developed many other rules, as well as stories that illustrated the rules and guidance. Rabbis had also interpreted this rule to include that an employer must find funds to pay the employees:

> "An employee must be paid with money (*Shulchan Aruch, [Shulchan Aruch, literally "the table" is an authoritative book provided numerous rules)* CM 336:1): one may not pay wages with goods or land. *Tosafos* (*Bava Kama* 9a) writes further that an employer who has no money is obligated to find the money with which to pay his employees. This ruling is cited by the *Shach* (*CM* 336:4), and the *Radvaz* (3:458) writes that it is a full obligation."[lvi]

Rabbis continue to interpret the rules, providing guidance to the modern day. One of the rules listed payment types. While years ago consumers had to pay in cash, in modern days, other types of payment may be valid:

> ""According to the reasoning mentioned by *Shach*, the manner of payment will depend on the normal expectations of a particular laborer. For a taxi cab, whose payment is almost always made in cash, the *mitzvah* of paying laborers would obligate a cash payment, and a check would not fulfill the *mitzvah*.
>
> If the driver is willing to accept a check the passenger would be saved from transgression; he would not, however, earn the credit of performing the *mitzvah*. If the check is paid against the driver's will, the passenger would be transgressing a Torah prohibition (*Teshuvos Ve-Hanhagos* vol. 3, sec. 470, part 3)"".[lvii]

In addition to listing the precise rules, Rabbis also provide stories (Aggadot) that demonstrate the reason for rules. The stories sometimes show the practices of famous Rabbis, and the Rabbis provide a shining example of righteous acts.

The following story illustrates the importance of paying employees timely, as well as noting that employees truly depend on the funds. The Rabbi could not truly focus on prayer (davening) until he was assured that the employees would receive prompt payment. The following demonstrates the importance of prompt payment, and how ethics with workers is more important than piety in worship:

> "The Arizal [Rabbi Yitzchak Luria, an important and well-known Rabbi known for mystical teachings] was exceptionally careful to pay his workers on time. Once, he realized that he didn't have the funds available to pay his worker. Nightfall, which is the deadline for the mitzvah of ....paying the worker the day he finishes his job, was quickly approaching. **The Arizal chose to try to borrow money to pay his worker, even though it meant not davening Minchah [afternoon prayer] on time.**
>
> According to many poskim [rulings], there is not an obligation to borrow money to pay a worker. Nevertheless, the Arizal gave priority to raising funds to pay a worker over davening at the appropriate time. Why?
>
> When we daven [pray], we stand before Hashem [the LORD] and declare that we are completely dependent on Hashem for all our needs. We beg Hashem to provide us with parnassah [livelihood], health and all our other desires. ... our employees rely on us for their parnassah. **They put in an honest day's work in order to be able to provide for themselves and their families.**
>
> **How can we daven to Hashem in good conscience, when we are letting down those who rely on us. If we do not provide for those who have served us well and deserve to be paid, how can we ask Hashem to provide us with what we have not earned and may not deserve?** There may be no technical obligation to borrow money to avoid the prohibition of *bal talin* [obligation to pay all debts on time]. But perhaps the Arizal felt that he could not daven until he fulfilled his personal obligations. Only after he had provided for those who were dependent on him was he ready to daven for his own needs and requests. " [lviii] (note – author's bold)

Promptly paying employees is actually considered so important that the requirement to promptly paying employees is actually more than an obligation; paying employees timely is a good deed (mitzvah). In fact, some people actually hired workers just to provide the mitzvah of paying employees on time. [lix]

In the modern days, prompt payment for vendors and employees remains important. In addition to paying employees for services, businesses also have a responsibility to pay for vendors (with increased rates of using independent contractors instead of employees, paying vendors is an even more important issue). Some employees can incur charges for late payment on various reimbursable expenses, such as travel. Paying employees' salary, as well as travel and reimbursing other expenses, is critical. Many people live month to month, having little in reserve. In fact, many people are so close to homelessness. For example, over a hundred million Americans are only a few months away from financial ruin: "If one of these households experiences a sudden loss of income, caused, for example, by a layoff or a medical emergency, it will fall below the poverty line."[lx] In October 2013, some employees did not receive payment, and a food bank in Arizona provided food to furloughed employees in the Grand Canyon. [lxi]

In modern days, due to the complexity of payment systems, paying vendors the same day that the vendors work on the "field" (in most industries, of course, the field can be anything from an actual office to a virtual office to a classroom) is very difficult, if not impossible. At the same point, making electronic payments can actually provide amounts into bank accounts fairly quickly.

Modern-day regulations about paying vendors is focused less on the carrot of doing a mitzvah (good deed) to instead the stick of paying interest for late payment. US federal agencies are required to pay vendors within 30 days (though accelerated payments within 15 days are required for smaller companies). Agencies will report on late payments in the agencies' publicly available financial statements. The goal is to decrease late payments. The Prompt Payment Act states:

> ""(ii) thirty days after receipt of a proper invoice for the amount of the payment due, if a specific date on which payment is due is not established by contract;""[lxii]

In addition to regulations that require paying vendors in a short period of times, regulations also require that federal agencies reimburse employees for travel expenses within 30 days. In fact, agencies must pay employees interest if the agencies pay the employees more than 30 days after the employees provide a valid travel claim.[lxiii]

In addition to rules for federal vendors, there are rules for state entities to pay vendors in a reasonable period of time. For example, California requires paying vendors within 45 days if vendors provide valid invoice. Virginia has regulations that require the state to pay vendors (i.e., vendors that perform work for the state government of Virginia). The Virginia Public Procurement Act, § 2.2-4347 through § 2.2-4356 states that a vendor must receive payment within 45 days:

> "The required payment date shall be either: (i) the date on which payment is due under the terms of the contract for the provision of the goods or services; or (ii) if a date is not established by contract, not more than forty-five days after goods or services are received or not more than forty-five days after the invoice is rendered, whichever is later."[lxiv]

If the state of Virginia doesn't pay vendors on time, Virginia is required to pay interest to the vendor. The interest rate is the standard rate used by commercial institutions (the prime rate): "The rate of interest charged a state agency pursuant to subsection A shall be the base rate on corporate loans (prime rate) at large United States money center commercial banks as reported daily in the publication entitled The Wall Street Journal." [lxv]

19. Good Deed in Employing People

The Talmud states that one of the most important aspects of a business is providing employment – not just perpetuating profit. Providing employment for people is a good deed

Following is an illustrative example, from a Chassidic (form of Orthodox Judaism) tale:

> "a wealthy businessman … decided to retire [and] wanted to close his factory, which was operating profitably, and spend the rest of his life studying the Talmud. He told the local rabbi about his plans, and he expected the rabbi to applaud his choice to become a man of great Talmudic wisdom. Instead, the rabbi was dismayed at the man's decision and asked "What will happen to all the workers you employ? How will they feed their families" The rabbi explained to the factory owner that **perhaps G-d gave him this wealth so that he would act as its trustee, and thus he had moral obligations to use it properly for the benefit of those in the community. His job was to provide jobs.**" [lxvi] (author's bold)

The Rabbinical goal of increasing employment is different from the attitude of many modern employers. A manager of one large employer that had the potential of providing hundreds with jobs stridently stated that the employer's goal was <u>not</u> to provide jobs. In a training class, the manager claimed "we are not a jobs service".

Businesses are under tremendous pressure to cut costs, especially during challenging economic times (e.g., a recession). Sometimes, businesses cut costs by cutting jobs, or getting rid of jobs via attrition (i.e., as people leave, not replacing the employees). Other times, businesses will cut jobs to meet shareholder expectations (e.g., obtain a net income that will meet estimates). Another method that businesses employ is only hiring temporary workers, thus providing flexibility to avoid long-term employment commitments (and consistent costs). The cost cutting measures often will often lead to ultimately decreasing career opportunities, cutting staff, or increasing workloads. The decrease in hiring could cause problems, including decreased morale. While some employers cannot employ a limited number of employees during economic duress, others simply fire employees just to meet earnings estimates.

The financial journalists, political pundits, and others sometimes compliment companies for firing employees en masse. For example, in the 1990s, the CEO "Chainsaw" Al Dunlap received compliments for firing tens of thousands of people. Al Dunlap would go to a new company, and then proceed to fire hundreds, if not thousands of people. The net income of the companies which he ran (e.g., Sunbeam) increased dramatically, leading to an increase in the stock price. Al Dunlap and others would make an assumption that cutting staff raised profits – thus providing an incentive to continue cutting jobs for his companies (and possibly for others). It seemed that firing people led to greater profits. The assumption (cutting jobs = short-term, and conceivably, long-term profitability), however, was not correct. Al Dunlap settled in a case against shareholders for $15 million[lxvii]. By the time the ex-CEO settled the case, however, damage was already done. People had already lost their jobs.

Firing people will not necessarily help a company. For example, a director a Bain & Company, one of the most prestigious consulting firms, noted that companies that did not downsize did better than companies that did downsize during an economic downturn ..... [lxviii]

Not all entities, however, decide to cut jobs and employment opportunities. The Biltmore Estate, a for-profit historical property [the former home of Vanderbilt), kept all jobs in the face of the "Great Recession". The CFO, Steve Watson stated:

> "When the Great Recession hit, the one instruction we got from our owners was to protect our employees' jobs. Salaries are our largest expense, so that was a huge obstacle that we had to overcome, but we did it. No full-time positions were eliminated. We are committed to our employees [and treat our employees] as our No. 1 asset. There are lots of historical landmarks and historical treasures, but I think it is our people that make Biltmore special." [lxix]

Not only do jobs provide financial support, they provide intangible value: "Whatever the job, it can give a sense of belonging, of being a contributor; an important part, however menial, of an organization with a bigger purpose, a valued part of society," wrote Tom Fryers, a professor. He continued: "Work can provide a structure for the day, week, and year without which life just drifts by."[lxx]

US federal policy provides an example of providing jobs. The US regulations provide several methods for legally staying in the United States and obtaining a valuable, actually priceless benefit – citizenship. One way in which someone from another nation can ultimately obtain citizenship is by investing in a new business and employing at least ten

Americans. The Department of Homeland Security's US Citizenship and Immigration Services states the following:

> Under a pilot immigration program first enacted in 1992 and regularly reauthorized since, certain EB-5 visas also are set aside for investors in Regional Centers designated by USCIS based on proposals for promoting economic growth.…."Create or preserve at least 10 full-time jobs for qualifying U.S. workers within two years (or under certain circumstances, within a reasonable time after the two-year period) of the immigrant investor's admission to the United States as a Conditional Permanent Resident. [lxxi]

Another example is a one company that made it a priority to pay employees, despite closing the building after a fire. In that way, the business studied the "Talmud and apply its teachings".[lxxii]

20. Marketing like a Mensch

Modern business makes the assumption that the seller will simply not admit the full truth. The seller will try their best to sell items, even if the seller doesn't fully disclose problems in a product, such as a computer, car, or an entire house. When buying a product, people are warned of the concept of buyer beware (caveat emptor). Yet, Jewish rules (Halachah) have a different approach on how to properly market with dignity, grace and honesty – the definition of a "mensch" (from "man" in Yiddish, means a person of high value and dignity; like a gentleman, but better).

The basic Jewish rule is that a seller has a duty to explain all defects in a product – this is above and beyond just disclosing what the law states: "All sales are presumed to have been made with the expectation that they are free of any defect. Therefore, selling an item without.... disclosing its defects is ... deception and is prohibited. [lxxiii] If a defective item is sold, the buyer has the right to void the sale and demand a refund.... ... "The seller is obligated to clearly disclose any defect in the items.. This disclosure must be specific." [lxxiv]

Jewish law (Halachah) also requires that the seller provide valid information – not only should a seller not explicitly lie, but the seller should also not indirectly deceive, based on information in the important book of rules, the Shulchan Aruch. Note that the buyer must only tell the actual truth, but also not deceive.

> "Misrepresentation is prohibited even if there is not actual lie. If an agent makes a statement that is designed to give the client a false impression, it is [deception] even if the agent did not actually say anything false". [lxxv]

Additionally, it is not allowed to make a product look better than the actual item. This could be analogous to sprucing up a car that is truly a "lemon": "One may not improve the appearance of a ... an animal, nor of old utensils, by making them appear to be new. One may, however, improve the appearance of new utensils, by polishing them, ironing them and beautifying them as much as necessary."[lxxvi]

This different approach (i.e., different from much of business world practice) shows the importance of not deceiving in any meaningful way, shape or form. While the approach may not result in short-term profit, it is the right thing to do.

21. Providing Bereavement Leave and Support

The Rabbis stated that an employee is deemed to have the right to take time off work for the death of the family member. The Talmud (in tractate Bava Metzia 77b) states the following:

> "If one engages a labourer, and in the middle of the day he [the labourer] learns that he has suffered a bereavement, or is smitten with fever: then if he is a time worker, he must pay him his wages;1 if a contract worker, he must pay him his contract price. Now, with whom does this agree? If with the Rabbis, why particularly if he learns that he has suffered a bereavement or is smitten with fever and so unfortunately compelled [to break the agreement]? Even if he is not compelled, surely the Rabbis maintain that the laborer has the advantage!"[lxxvii] .

Note that the Rabbis created this guidance that required bereavement leave over 1,000 years ago! While bereavement leave is standard (many companies and agencies provide such leave), it does show the value of supporting employees. For example, some large employers are provided bereavement leave of up to three days.[lxxviii] Providing bereavement leave can, of course, help employees in a time of dire need and depression. And not providing the bereavement leave could make employees bitter – and motivate employees to eventually leave. With a "war for talent" for the most qualified employees, it is important to have benefits that keep employees happy.

22. Thou Shalt Not Poach Employees

It is important to maintain proper boundaries in business. The following is an interpretation of a Torah text is that a company should not poach employees from other companies: "Do not encroach on the boundary of your neighbour (in connection with poaching employees) - *Deuteronomy 19:14*." ^{lxxix}

This is interesting example of the depth of Torah rules. While the Torah disallows stealing, the Torah also contains a rule that is similar to stealing – getting close to taking someone that one does not truly own – encroaching. In a similar manner, it is not valid to take another company's employees in an aggressive manner. Of course, people change companies often, but poaching is a higher level, especially for those with sought-after skills.

23. Providing a Sabbatical

In many religious congregations, it is common to provide clergy with a sabbatical. For example, a Rabbi explains the importance of providing a year-long sabbatical to Rabbis. The term sabbatical (from the same root as *Shabbas,* for the seventh day) is actually derived from a section of the Hebrew Bible, in Leviticus 25:2-4:

> Speak unto the children of Israel, and say unto them, When ye come into the land which I give you, then shall the land keep a sabbath unto the LORD.
> Six years thou shalt sow thy field, and six years thou shalt prune thy vineyard, and gather in the fruit thereof;
> but in the seventh year shall be a sabbath of rest unto the land, a sabbath for the LORD: thou shalt neither sow thy field, nor prune thy vineyard.

A Rabbi explains the importance of the sabbatical:

> "It is upon these verses that the idea of a sabbatical year for professionals has been built. Just as we are told to let our land lay fallow in order to rest the land after six years of growth, we understand that a valued professional and teacher too should have the chance to revitalize after six years of harvesting their creative fruits. ... There is a great deal that we can learn from this agricultural idea in terms of our own synagogue communities. In communities that practice this land sabbatical year, the "shemitah" year, they are aware that it is coming and must make provisions for this year. They are aware of the biblical cycle and they build their agricultural cycle upon this progression. So too in our communities we should understand that these seasons are a part of a good use of our resources. We need to treasure the professionals who help us to grow up sacred community and we should nurture them for the good harvest that our community will yield if we properly attend to the growth and wellbeing of the resources we have in our communities." [lxxx]

In the USA, it has been common in academia to take a paid leave of absence. In addition to educational entities, some for-profit companies provide sabbaticals to take a break from the job to focus on other efforts. The employees were able to take several weeks leave (paid time) from their job. Large US companies, such as Intel, have provided sabbaticals. Sometimes, the companies provide benefits but not pay in the sabbatical (such as the large consultancy, Accenture). Some large accounting firms provide sabbaticals, which have provided employees the opportunity to go on extended travel, serve the community, or work personal projects. [lxxxi] One American consultancy had provided sabbaticals to employees who had worked for several years.

In a world in which it can be challenging to keep the best workers, providing sabbaticals encourages people to stay in one company. For example, an employee with a high-level clearance and strong technical skills might have more motivation to stay several years, if the employee knows he/she would get a sabbatical after working for a certain number of years. A staffing company in the DC area also offers month-long sabbaticals to employees that have worked for five years. The *Washingtonian* magazine actually listed this staffing company as one of the Top 50 best places to work. .[lxxxii] Forbes created a list of the 13 best perks in business, and listed the sabbatical as one of the best perks. Forbes stated that the large consultancy Deloitte "Gives generous sabbaticals, either four unpaid weeks a year to do anything or, every 36 months, 3-6 months at 40% pay to volunteer or do career development."[lxxxiii] Hence, one can see the importance of providing sabbaticals, as a way to keep employees, and to provide positive press.

Taking a break is so important that in Australia, employers must provide a two month break after ten years of service, and then breaks after each two months – "After their first ten years with a company, they get two months off (with pay). It's another month every five years after that.[lxxxiv]

The Rabbis were right on sabbaticals. Providing an extended, paid break is an effective tool to keep employees. Many companies now claim to struggle to keep and engage excellent employees. The sabbatical can also provide great publicity.

24. Teshuvah – Returning Employees to the Correct Path

Jewish ethics and practices emphasize the importance of empowering people to change. One of the most important Rabbis, Rashi, noted the following in his interpretation of Leviticus 25:35:

> "Do not let your fellow slip down until they fall completely, for then it will be difficult to raise them; rather, strengthen your fellow as they begin to fall. To what is this comparable? To a burden upon a donkey. While it is still on the donkey, one person can hold it and set it in place. If it falls to the earth, even five people cannot set it back. Rashi, Leviticus 25:35 (cf. Torat Kohanim, Sifre Behar, Chapter 5)" [lxxxv]

For example, an employee might make inappropriate comments at work. This could occur for a variety of reasons including emotions from personal stress, lack of self-control or even drug addiction. By Jewish law, the employer would provide the employee a warning that the employee would understand. Note the focus is not the manager thinking the manager properly provided the message – the employer is responsible for ensuring that the employee understands the message. If the employee does not fully understand the message, the employee is not responsible, and should not suffer disciplinary action. In many cases, employers fail to communicate in ways that the employee understands, especially for employees that the employers think are not meeting expectations. The employee would then have the option to stop his/her behavior, as one modern Rabbi explained: "Even though the worker is now only changing his actions because of external pressure, Jewish tradition affirms the value of a change in behavior even when it is not accompanied by a change in character." [lxxxvi]

One of the harshest punishments any employee can suffer is losing their job. Firing an employee can result in lost income, lost benefits and lost pride. An employee can go into a depression when fired. In fact, during times of recession, some people losing jobs actually are driven to drink (and drink too much). A recent study showed that for each one percentage "increase in the state unemployment rate corresponded to a nearly 17% increase in cases of alcoholism or alcohol abuse and a 35% increase in rates of drunk driving." [lxxxvii] Being out of work for a long time can make it harder to obtain another job. In fact, having a long period of unemployment traditionally looks very bad on a resume, and can lead to not even getting an interview. For decades, hiring officials have been concerned about gaps in a resume.

One basic premise is Jewish idea of a sin and a sinner. In Judaism, someone who is sinning is simply on the wrong path. Teshuvah means going back into the correct (and righteous) path. The concept is that a sinner can change, can go on the right path. This includes providing employees the option of turning on to the right path, providing a different way when employees make mistakes. This includes a long-term option of sending employees on the right path in their careers.

For example, one employer had an employee that struggled in a work assignment. Instead of firing the employee, or creating a rating form that would simply provide fodder (rationale) to latter fire the employee, the employer provided candid counsel to the employee. A manager told the employee that the present assignment was not good for the employee, and found another assignment that better met the employee's skillset. The employee worked for several more years, doing well overall in the tasks, and becoming a productive member of the organization.

There are limits, however. Going back on the right path is not always an option. In the Torah, there are numerous instances in which G-d (Hashem, which means the name) enacts punishment on a group of people, and the people cannot make amends – it is too late. The Sodomites were one such group of people. The major sin of the Sodomites was a disgusting treatment of strangers. In Genesis, two angels visited Lot, a person living in Sodom. Lot very quickly tells the angels to go into his house. The Sodomites wanted to have sexual relations with the angels, and tried to break into the house. Eventually Hashem destroys all of Sodom, as there are simply not enough (not even ten) righteous people in the entire town (Genesis 18 – 19). The lesson is that there are some, extreme cases, where employees are corrupt, and will not go to the right path. Bernie Madoff is probably a good example, of someone who has sinned so harshly, without any concern for others, that he was permanently punished for his actions.

In the workplace, employees should also not have endless opportunities. Rabbinic law states that a "negligent" employee may be fired after the employee was been "negligent three times. At that point the [employee] is considered an unreliable worker. However, the worker must be warned each time that the employee will be fired if [the] behavior continues"[lxxxviii]. Hence, by Jewish law, employees must be given clear warnings each time. The goal is not to punish the employees, but in many ways to improve (or in modern views, re-direction).

25. Though Shalt Treat Employees with Dignity Upon Leaving

A wise person once said that class is treating people who <u>cannot</u> help you. Providing the soon to be ex-employees (especially employees the company perceives as weak and unhelpful) various benefits shows tremendous class and kindness. Additionally, one of the most important Rabbis, Hillel, has a wise quote (years before the Golden Rule). When asked to explain Judaism while standing on one foot, the Rabbi states: 'That which is hateful unto you do not do to your neighbor. This is the whole of the Torah, The rest is commentary. Go forth and study.'[lxxxix]

Therefore, devising a way to provide employees sufficient time to look for another job, recommending other employers, and devising a roadmap are all great ideas. For example, some large accounting or law firms will recommend an employee leave ("counseling out"), though not specifically asking the employee to resign.

On the corollary, one organization fired staff who had been working at the organization for years. The manager told the staff to "have a good life". The organization provided no help in obtaining another position. A coworker wisely commented "Have a good life. How is [she or he] supposed to have a good life [without having a job]?"

Providing a dignified way of leaving is very important. For example, one of the most important rabbis, Maimonides, notes that the highest form of charity is helping someone truly help themselves; and providing advice and guidance to employees before employers fire the employees is helpful.

Treating employees with a lack of proper dignity or respect, however, even lead to lawsuits:

> "One common employer mistake that leads to employee lawsuits is failing to treat terminated employees with dignity....Escorting the employee out in an obvious or heavy-handed manner without allowing them to gather personal belongings, badmouthing the employee with co-workers, deducting or withholding from the employee's final paycheck, and providing negative references can all prompt the employee to seek revenge through lawsuits....A related mistake is where the employer threatens the employee to resign voluntarily, trying to escape lawsuits for unlawful terminations. Chances are this would only add to the chances of a lawsuit."[xc]

Therefore, providing a path of employment for ex-employees is not just the right thing to do, it can be financially sound. If an employer can take all steps needed to find employees a job somewhere else, it can help save face and save money.

26. Though Shalt Properly Treat Employees after Leaving an Organization

Not only should an organization treat employees well before leaving, but also treat employees well after the employees stop working. One example of treating employees fairly is severance, guaranteed payment for work that the employee has already performed. Some countries provide numerous rules on severance. There are many situations that will require severance, such as poor health, poor health in the family member and other reasons. [xci] For example, in Israel "severance [must] be paid at the rate of one month per year of employment for all employees in almost every field of labor[xcii]. A Jewish court of law (Beit Din) also interpreted that rules of severance can also be based on customs.

> "Severance as an enforceable obligation can only be explained in Jewish law as a custom that has gained wide acceptance, and thus develops a force of its own. In the words of the Israeli Rabbinical court, "the custom of paying severance has support in the text of the Torah and the Halacha and is thus a proper custom." [xciii]

Class is helping those who cannot help one in any meaningful way. Helping an ex-employee (especially with an ex-employee who cannot help the company in any reasonable way) is actually similar to helping the dead – it is helping someone who cannot benefit you. Following is an example of the mitzvah of helping the dead:

> "*Chevra Kadisha* means "Sacred Society," but it is more commonly translated as "Jewish Burial Society." The tradition of having a *Chevra Kadisha*goes goes back more than 2000 years (in Stamford, more than 100 years). As Jewish communities formed throughout the world, a *Chevra Kadisha* was one of the first groups to be organized in each community. It was, and is, considered a great honor to be a member, and its work is considered nothing less than holy. Their work is called *chesed shel emes*, the ultimate good deed, since they can *never be repaid for their kindness.* "[xciv]

In some entities, however, management sometimes shows a lack of respect or dignity to ex-employers. For example, one very large employer decided to fire an employee (let's call the employee "Jim"). The employer had a huge profit margin, a steady stream of near-guaranteed revenue, and limited risk. The economy was not strong. The employee struggled to find another job and did not have sufficient time to find a comparable professional position, though struggled financially and took and worked in a much lower-paying job. The employee needed to support a family, including a child. Another employee noted that the ex-employee had several personal items still in the office where Jim used to work. The other employee asked the ex-employee's manager, asking "where should we send Jim's stuff?" The manager rudely said "I don't care about [Jim's] stuff".

Other managers have had similar responses in far too many other organizations, seeing clearing out the ex-employee's stuff an errand to complete as soon as possible, without caring about the personal property. This shows a lack of class, and denies the employee the proper dignity that every employee and ex-employee deserves. Just as a reasonable person would not spit in a grave, an employer should not throw away personal effects or otherwise disrespect an ex-employer.

27. Charging Reasonable Interest Rates

Traditional Jewish rules prohibit charging interest, in detailed rules known as *ribbis.* Rabbis have created a complex work-around, which effectively will allow for Jews to charge for the investment.

While there are ways to work around *ribbis*, Jews are not allowed to charge "exorbitant rates" for certain short-term loans. According to Halachah, charging higher rates, even that a lender may consider "appropriate" at the "level of risk involved in these transactions...does not mitigate the prohibition of ribis." [xcv]

Charging reasonable interest rates continues to be an issue. Subprime mortgage rates created great deal of stress for many Americans. "Payday" loans were also very controversial. In many communities, a lender would provide a short-term loan for someone's pay at a very high rate. Other examples including providing "instant tax refunds", in which companies would actually take 10% of the tax refund up front, or similar methods could cost hundreds of dollars. [xcvi]

In this case, it is not right to charge incredibly high rates of interest, especially if the consumers would be unaware of the true interest rates. Recent regulation has tried to minimize these high rates.

28. Though Shalt Pay the Market Prices

In the secular market, the practice is sometimes to pay as little as possible for goods and services, while charging customers as much as possible (hence making the highest possible profit). This includes charging above-market prices, and assuming that the consumers don't know the market. Consumers will try to find bargains, situations in which the seller simply does not realize the true value of products. Companies might try to pay very low salaries to people, including salaries below the prevailing market rate. A small business, for example, could pay some administrative professionals (who have several skills, including fluency in Spanish and English) at less than $10 an hour, though the prevailing market rate is closer to $14-15.

In Jewish Law, however, the rule is an employer must pay at the market rate and the consumer must pay at a market rate. These laws apply "regardless of how higher or low the seller's profit margin may be." In fact, if an item in a store is underpriced, one is obligated to inform the storeowner: "Buying the item without notifying the owner of the item's true value is [prohibited], even though the merchant made the mistake on his own." [xcvii] An example of this case would be a vending machine that charges $1.25 for an item, yet due to an error, one could buy the item (e.g., soda) for just $0.25. Instead of taking advantage of the situation, and buying more cans, one would be "forbidden" to buy the cans in this machine. [xcviii]

Paying market prices is also required for employers. An employer that underpays workers is violating prohibition for paying proper rates, according to many Rabbis.[xcix]

29. Thou Shalt Be Kind to the Environment

The Jewish texts (e.g., the Torah) have a relatively positive view toward nature. Judaism has an entire holiday devoted to trees – Tu B'Shvat. [c] This holiday is the New Year for Trees. The Bible includes passages that emphasize the importance of maintaining the trees. Even during warfare (including sections that command the Israelites to fight with courage against their enemies), Deuteronomy 20:19 states that the Israeli armies must not cut down trees (at least those that produce food), including if the takes a long time to conquer a city:

> When thou shalt besiege a city a long time, in making war against it to take
> it, thou shalt not destroy the trees thereof by forcing an axe against them:
> for thou mayest eat of them, and thou shalt not cut them down (for the tree
> of the field *is* man's *life*) to employ *them* in the siege:

The Torah thus states that even in the perils of war, Jews should save trees and protect the resources, including for future production.

Some companies have caused environmental harm, such as the harm caused by oil spills (e.g., BP). Therefore, it would not be right to hurt or harm the environment.

30. Thou Shalt be Kind to Animals

Judaism emphasizes the dignity that animals deserve. In the well-known story, when a flood destroyed the world, G-d made sure to keep two of all species of animals, showing that all species are precious. Not being cruel to animals is considered one of the seven rules that Jews think everyone (Jews and gentiles) should follow (Noahide" laws).[ci] Also, Judaism teaches that one should feed animals first, before feeding humans:

> Based on Deuteronomy 11:15, "And I will give grass in the fields for thy cattle and thou shall eat and be satisfied," the Talmud teaches that a person should not eat or drink before first providing for his or her animals. [cii]

Some businesses have decided to embrace the entire of not just following the complex rules of being kosher, but also being "green" kosher. Green kosher can also include providing animal rights.[ciii]

Some people have decided to be vegan to protect animals, as a method to not kill animals directly, or otherwise cause harm. Some think that the egg industry causes pain the chickens, while the dairy industry is very painful to cows. Some Rabbis claim that the Jewish rules of proper killing of animals was a compromise, as G-d wanted humans to not eat animal products, while many people wanted to eat any animal. So the compromise was to limit the animals that one could eat.

31. Though Shalt Not Bully Their Subordinates

In the Mishnah Torah (book of laws), Maimonides writes the following sage words about bullying:

> "Verbally abusing a person is more severe than taking unfair advantage of him financially. For the latter can be repaid, while the former can never be repaid. The latter involves only the person's possessions, while the former involves his person."[civ]

A person's pride in this case has a large, almost priceless, value. In many offices, managers can verbally abuse staff, which is a type of bullying. While the media has focused on anti-bullying efforts for children, bullying adults can be just as pernicious. In fact, in some ways, bullying is even worse in the working world. A child can often run to his/her teacher or parents, who can help fight the battles. Yet, in general, an employee cannot run to parents or spouses, and must try to work with the employer's (often subjective) resources. And the employer's resource, (e.g., HR) works for management, which could cause a conflict of interest.

Though bullying is technically prohibited, in some places a cruel manager can cause many problems. An expert noted the following: "Bullying in the workplace is something that's often overlooked," said Jennette Pokorny, COO of human resources service provider EverNext HR. "People should come to work and feel safe. You don't want to allow something minor to escalate."[cv]

Bullying is even a problem in the NFL. In 2013, the coach of the Miami Dolphins admitted fault for allowing the Dolphins to reach a "toxic point." Bullying within the Dolphins had a large negative impact, costing millions of dollars and draft picks. The Dolphins will work with a variety of groups to change the environment to implement "a curriculum which....educates athletes on the standard code of conduct, appropriate use of language, and the elimination of disrespectful and unacceptable behavior in sports..." [cvi] Bullying can hurt employees both directly and indirectly. One study found that people who were bullied in the office actually were more likely to take prescription drugs. [cvii]

Bullying is rampant: "Startlingly, over 80 percent of respondents stated that they believe that bullying is a serious problem in the workplace". Yet, less than a quarter of American companies "do anything about workplace bullying." Workplace bullying includes others swearing, shouting at employees, humiliating employees, and provided "unwarranted or invalid criticism and blame without factual justification.""[cviii]

Not only does Jewish Halachah have some rules – Rabbis continue to promulgate interpretations (*"responsa"*)". Rabbi Jill Jacobs states the following:

> "...Jewish employers are obligated to treat their workers with dignity and respect. This obligation should include, but should not be limited to, prohibitions against publicly yelling at, mocking, or otherwise embarrassing workers" [cix]

32. <u>Work / Life Balance – Employer Responsibilities</u>

Major Jewish texts emphasize the importance of providing employees sufficient time for life events, such as spouses and children. The Rabbis also mention issues with having a lack of work life balance.

In the Hebrew Bible, Deuteronomy 24:5 states an important rule about work/life balance, emphasizing that a newly married couple must have time at home. The context is important, as the Jewish people fought in numerous wars to establish and control the nation of ancient Israel. Despite the wars that the Israelites fought against nations in the Near East, the Torah still contains the rule that required Jews to stay in their homes, to make the first year of marriage wonderful. Each marriage then is of upmost importance.

> "When a man hath taken a new wife, he shall not go out to war, neither shall he be charged with any business: *but* he shall be free at home one year, and shall cheer up his wife which he hath taken."

The corporate world, however, sometimes lacks this work-life balance. An executive at a consulting firm called an employee to ask for information or a work product. The employee was returning from the funeral. The executive continued to ask for the information for the PowerPoint slides for the work effort. The employee said that she was just getting back from a funeral, and the executive insisted on getting work done on the slides immediately – it was not acceptable to wait.

A lack of work-life balance can cause huge problems, as sometimes companies focus in pursuit of profit and production instead of people's health. An example of people not providing proper work-life balance occurs in the beginning of the Bible, in one of the first groups of people to live in the world. In Genesis Chapter 11, verses 1-9, a group of people tried to build a tower so high that the tower (the Tower of Babel) would reach the heavens. At the time that the people were building the tower, the people living in the world spoke just one language. G-d was so upset with the people that G-d created numerous languages for the people, so that the people can longer communicate. G-d also physically scattered the people around the world. One of the Rabbinical stores emphasizer that the people who built the tower had a lack of concern for human life. The tower becomes more important than lives:

> Many, many years were passed in building the tower. It reached so great a height that it took a year to mount to the top. A brick was, therefore, more precious in the sight of the builders than a human being. If a man fell down, and met his death, none took notice of it, but if a brick dropped, they wept, because it would take a year to replace it. So intent were they upon

accomplishing their purpose that they would not permit a woman to interrupt herself in her work of brick-making when the hour of travail came upon her. Molding bricks she gave birth to her child, and, tying it round her body in a sheet, she went on molding bricks.[cx]

Companies (and other organizations) sadly sometimes operate in the same principles of the Tower of Babel. In 2013, a video production assistant tragically died while trying to film a movie on a bridge. The movie crew did not have permission to be on the bridge – the video was supposed to include a hospital bed on a bridge. A train actually ran over the hospital bed, and shrapnel killed a 27 year old camera woman:

> While Gilliard, Jones and the rest of the crew were preparing to start filming, multiple witnesses told "20/20," two trains passed by. After the second train, the crew moved out on the bridge to place a hospital bed and the camera on the train trestle, multiple witnesses told "20/20. ..Then, someone asked what to do if a train was spotted.

> "[Someone said], 'You have 60 seconds to get off the track.' I was more or less, '60 seconds to get off the track?'" Gilliard said. "And I started praying. I'm mad at myself because I didn't say something." ..The owner of the land adjacent to the bridge had allegedly given the production crew permission to be there and had also reportedly told them that only two trains would use the track that day.

> There were no railroad officials or medical help present on set, ... " nor was the film's location manager, Charley Baxter. He hadn't been able to obtain permission from the railroad to film on the trestle bridge. Baxter emailed the railroad's refusal to producers just before 11 a.m. that day.[cxi]

In a situation that sadly seems to show an eerily parallel story to mythical tower of Babel, some people have rumored that some employers in a developing country decided not to use fake glass to save funds, thus literally hurting employees.

Another prominent example is the Ford Pinto. In the late 60s and early 70s, the Ford Pinto had a flaw in the fuel design. It would have cost just $11 a car to make literally lifesaving changes. For a small investment in designing and building cards, Ford would have likely prevented 180 deaths. Ford made a decision that the cost of re-design would not outweigh the benefit of the savings. It would cost $49.5 million on "deaths, injuries and car damages, while it would cost $137 million on redesign. So Ford argued that "risk/benefit" analysis justified the decision not to redesign the car." [cxii]

Currently, companies will often boast of work/life balance. For example, the Partnership for Public Service recently surveyed federal entities about work satisfaction/dissatisfaction. One of the elements is work/life balance. The federal employers on the top of the list will obtain good press, while the laggards will receive increased criticism, prompting senior management action (or rather, reaction). Vault.com lists the best places for work / life balance[cxiii]. Not all companies include in their goals work life balance; one consulting companies refused to include work-life balance, internally acknowledged that the company simply lacked work-life balance.

While overall companies mostly seem to extol and prioritize work-life balance, in practice for-profit companies, non-profit companies and governmental employees seem not truly put families first. In a distinct contrast to the rule of providing a sufficient time to plant a vineyard before going to war, an employee desperately looked for a substitute instructor so that the employee could attend her own wedding. She had to get a substitute teacher; otherwise she would experience problems at work. In another situation, a pregnant woman didn't want to go to teach a group exercise, as she was concerned she would faint. She (the "instructor") was feeling dizzy, and had very bad "morning" (really all day) sickness as she was pregnant. She told her manager, and her manager still stridently required her to teach the class. The instructor had to get a sub, even though she was sick and probably should not have worked. The instructor even had her husband go to the class to help support her in case there were any issues. The instructor stopped teaching the class, and will not return to the employer after she has a baby.

There are times when the work stops, when life priorities should take over. In one consulting company, an employee called his manager, telling his manager about his Aunt's impending death. The Aunt was a loving mother, sister, and grandmother. While the manager was busy with numerous deadlines, the manager made the time to ask "is everything OK." The employee said that he was not OK. The employee stated that he would need to take a week off work to attend a funeral. The manager provided a full listing of others who would back-up his (or change it all to first person) training. Others in the group performed the training.

An employee was working, stating that his wife's stomach had sharp pains. The spouse was concerned about numerous medical issues, such as appendicitis. The manager quickly approved, with no issues. While the above scenario seems very obvious, it is not so commonplace.

Another company's management, however, acted in a much worse way. A group fitness instructor had a medical emergency, and needed to go to the urgent care. Her husband took her the urgent care for medical treatment. The employee contacted her boss, stating that she was in in urgent care. The situation was so dire that the employee was on an IV. The employee's husband contacted the manager. The manager asked the husband to find a substitute teacher. The husband contacted numerous other fitness instructors - from the urgent care. This caused tremendous stress.

A large (one of the "Big Four" – these are the four largest accounting firms in the world) accounting / consulting firm provides an example of great work-life balance policies. The large firm Ernst & Young (E&Y) announced that new mothers and fathers would get 16 weeks of paid maternity/paternity leave. E&Y provided other benefits to couples having children a variety of ways. E&Y clearly was making a point, and wanted to provide better benefits than competitors:

> EY debuted a new parental leave policy on Wednesday that will expand its employee benefits to up to 16 fully-paid weeks for all new moms and dads in the U.S. The professional services firm also took the subtext of most splashy parental benefits announcement and made it explicit, essentially saying, "Our policy blows our competitors' benefits out of the water."

> The announcement, which also revealed that EY will offer up to $25,000 per same or opposite sex couple for fertility, surrogacy, adoption, and egg freezing services, includes much of the standard discussion of how the new policies will benefit employees and strengthen the company's workforce.

> But it also throws down the gauntlet for other professional services firms. The headline on a press release declares, "U.S. firm now leads professional services in paid time off for new parents," and the company notes that the new policies make EY a "1st mover in equalizing parental leave benefits for men and women among the Big Four, Accenture, IBM and other professional services firms."[cxiv]

Granting leave for life events is another important element. An employee had asked for leave to go to Disney world. The manager rejected the request, stating that the employee needed to work on high priority efforts. The employee that was denied vacation remembered the situation, and always provided vacation to his employees.

In another entity, an employee asked for leave to visit the employee's adult child, who lived in Africa. It would take several days to get the Africa, and there was a limited time window to visit. The employee requested the leave. The manager disapproved the leave, asking to go for a few days to Africa (instead of two weeks), cancel the trip, or move the trip several months. The manager stated she had to "make the hard decisions around here", and needed coverage for what the manager considered important work priorities.

While coworkers do well on understanding life events of marriage, childbirth, and death, it's also important to provide support.

> Part of work-life balance is also maintain help, which can also help the company. In modern day, this is an issue, even metro has been studying methods of employees sleeping enough. Recently, the Washington, DC. Metro Authority

("Metro") researched employees obtaining sufficient sleep. Metro was struggling with employee issues. In many cases, the employees worked so many hours that the employees actually fell asleep while performing their duties, including even driving a bus. [cxv]

A separate study released last year found that employees in safety-critical jobs worked longer hours than allowed. And the study found Metro did not have any limits on the consecutive number of days worked. Earlier this year the transit agency released data showing cameras on Metro buses found 67 drivers fell asleep at the wheel in a 19-month period.

Therefore, work-life balance, from the principles of allowing employees time to help their family and other important commitments, remains important. Jewish law notes the importance of providing sufficient time to take care of one's family and house. And employers should try similar efforts to help employees. The work-life balance can literally help employees keep their livelihood – and their own life.

33. Providing Proper Punishments – and Notice

The Bible is full of information about proper punishments, providing a detailed listing of Israelite actions and G-d's expected reactions. The Bible clearly states that if Jews follow commandments, Jews will experience prosperity. If the Jews do not follow G-d's rules, the Jewish people will suffer; the Bible lists the punishments. The punishments are severe. Another example is in the Prophets, in the Book of Isaiah, Chapter 1, Verses 18-20, which show the ability to change, as well as punishments:

> "Come now, and let us reason together, saith the LORD: though your sins
> be as scarlet, they shall be as white as snow; though they be red like
> crimson, they shall be as wool.
> If ye be willing and obedient, ye shall eat the good of the land:
> but if ye refuse and rebel, ye shall be devoured with the sword: for the
> mouth of the LORD hath spoken it.

The Rabbis also provide various punishments for incorrect actions. One Rabbi named Chazal states that workers should not pay for damages that are accidental, such as a porter who "drops an item". The Rabbi noted that "people would not accept such difficult and low-paying jobs if they had liability". In fact, even in cases that do not qualify for this exemption, it is appropriate for an employer to forgive any damage that [the] workers cause, if it was caused by the workers' negligence[cxvi] In some companies, if an employee damages equipment, the employee may be fully liable and harshly punished – for an honest mistake. In some organizations, if low level clerks cannot balance the cash register to cash received, the employee will pay for any imbalance.

Sometimes, employees may make mistakes, unaware and uninformed about company policies. Or the employee is unable to interpret complex and convoluted policies. The employees may then be dealt harshly, including financial penalties, forced unpaid leave, lack of future promotional opportunities, or termination. Based on Rabbinic recommendations, many employer policies are not proper if the employer does not properly communicate in ways the employees can understand.

34. Thou Shalt Not Take or Give Bribes

Jewish law recognizes the sinfulness and long term damaged due to bribes. For example, Isaiah, Chapter 1, Verse 21-24, describes a terrible city that has gone on the wrong path, which includes thievery, treating orphans and widows poorly, and giving and accepting bribes.

Bribes are in many ways one of the worst sins. Bribes can result in a lack of justice; this includes police, other government officials and regulators looking the other way. In the Jewish Day of Atonement (Yom Kippur), Jews are to ask forgiveness for the people they have wronged. To obtain forgiveness, Jews are supposed to ask for forgiveness three times. There are, however, five sins that are particularly bad, for which one cannot receive forgiveness, as it is:

> "...**impossible for the sinner to do complete Teshuvah**, for they are sins against another person, but the sinner does not know against whom he has sinned, to whom he must make restitution, and whom he must ask forgiveness." ... "accepting a bribe to bend the law, for one can <u>never</u> appraise the ramifications and loss caused by bribery, and will therefore not be able to rectify the manner"[cxvii] (author's bold)

Bribes continue to be a huge issue. Some corporations continue to accept bribes. Large accounting firms and law firms make a great deal of money in identifying fraud, which often includes bribes. In the United States, the federal government has various mechanisms to decrease bribes. There are harsh penalties to bribe a federal official. There are many regulations disallowing fraud. Numerous professionals have a certification in fraud detection. Employees receive ethics training, an entire field that works with fraud (e.g., forensic accounting; Certified Fraud Examiners). Despite the safeguards, companies and individuals continue to pay bribes.

For example, a US-based company admitted to bribes to put ATMs in banks overseas:

> A company that makes ATMs and other bank security services has agreed to pay $48.1 million to settle charges that it bribed foreign government officials and forged records to put its ATMs in banks overseas. The Justice Department and the Securities and Exchange Commission (SEC) announced on Tuesday that it had reached an agreement with Ohio-based Diebold Inc. over a series of bribes that stretches back to 2005. According to the charges, Diebold bribed officials in China and Indonesia with gifts, entertainment, travel and money totaling $1.75 million from 2005-2010. The company tried to disguise the payments by routing them through third parties and claiming that some trips were for training. Among those trips was a two-week vacation for eight officials at a Chinese government-owned bank to stops including Paris, Rome, Munich and Venice. "A bribe is a

70

bribe, whether it's a stack of cash or an all-expense-paid trip to Europe," Scott Friestad, an associate director in the SEC's enforcement division, said in a statement on Tuesday. "Public companies must be held accountable when they break the law to influence government officials with improper payments or gifts."[cxviii]

Sadly, bribes are so prevalent, even in organizations in which employees receive training to avoid bribes. A bribery scandal erupted while I was writing the first edition of this book! Employees in the US Navy may have been bribed by a foreign official. The foreign official may have even been bribed with prostitutes: "The U.S. Navy is being rocked by a bribery scandal that federal investigators say has reached high into the officer corps and exposed a massive overbilling scheme run by an Asian defense contractor that provided prostitutes and other kickbacks."[cxix]

In January 2014, a federal indictment started against former Virginia governor Bob McDonnell. The governor was at one point close to being a Vice Presidential candidate, and had a chance at eventually being a President. Yet, a huge scandal erupted near the end of his term. The indictment included many charges, including a company allegedly giving money to pay off credit card debts, pay $20,000 towards McDonnell's daughter's wedding, and pay for other items. McDonnell was found guilty: "The McDonnells were convicted on nearly all the counts involving doing favors for wealthy vitamin executive Jonnie Williams in exchange for more than $165,000 in gifts and loans that they admitted taking.""[cxx]

Bribery remains an issue not only in the United States, but in the entire world, and a quarter of people in a survey took bribes:

> More than 1 in 4 people around the world reported having paid a bribe in the previous year when interacting with key public institutions and services, according to Transparency International's Global Corruption Barometer 2013.Fifty-three percent of respondents in the Barometer survey thought corruption had increased a lot over the past two years.[cxxi]

In September 2014, a huge company as fined by China for millions in bribes: "China fined GlaxoSmithKline Plc <GSK.L> a record 3 billion yuan ($489 million) on Friday for paying bribes to doctors to use its drugs":[cxxii], This is clearly an issue that requires constant vigilance.

35. Though Shalt Place Employees in Proper Roles

The Bible states that one should not place a stumbling block before the blind, which seems fairly obvious. A Rabbi keenly interprets this statement more broadly: "Placing a stumbling block before the blind has never been limited to a purely literal meaning. This concept is considered a prohibition on placing people in context where they would be unable to cope with their responsibilities and temptation." [cxxiii] This makes sense. In fact, in the Bible, Hashem (the "name" a word for the LORD) often will select people who have the right skills to do their mission. As Moses was not a great a speaker, his brother Aaron was his spokesperson. Rarely did Hashem select a leader who was set up for failure, who lacked the talent to do his (or her) job well.

Some wise leaders know how to not setup people for failure. This includes creating an optimum "startling lineup." One sage wrestling coach had a team whose staring wrestler was injured. A freshmen wrestler could have started (Varsity). The wrestler, though, was fairly small for the weight class and inexperienced. Instead of risking injury to the wrestler or an uncompetitive loss, the coach just took a forfeit (didn't put anyone into the match), and instead had the wrestler have a Junior Varsity (lower level than Varsity) match, for better experience. The coach would not setup the wrestler for failure, yet still provided an opportunity to compete. The wrestler eventually improved, and wound up being a successful high school and college wrestler.

In this context, businesses should place employees in appropriate roles that would avoid the employees being put into temptation. Managers will generally know about their employees' strengths and weaknesses, and should be able to make the proper assignments. While employees have a responsibility to act properly, the employer can prevent issues from occurring by placing employees in the proper roles and assignments. It is important not to set up the employee for failure. One entity put an employee in a position where she had to be in the office every day, yet it would have been better if the employee was able to work from home due to physical challenges. Placing employees in proper roles can be beneficial:

> "…people do best at the work that they enjoy doing. You, as a manager, have some control over the situation simply by how you manage. …More importantly, be sensitive to the skills and interests of your employees as you assign them to jobs. Try to put people in jobs that suit them. Put the dreamer in charge of creative tasks. Put the detail-oriented individual on tasks with more structure. Don't put your introverted loner into customer service." [cxxiv]

Providing the appropriate roles can be very helpful. An employee struggled in a position, and the manager wisely assessed the skillset that the employee had, and put an employee in a role where the employee would succeed.

36. Though Shall Use Proper Weights

It is paramount to properly measure the asset purchased and sold. The Bible states that each individual must ensure that his scales and weights are accurate (Leviticus 19:36). Proverbs (part of the Writings that contains timeless wisdom) 11:1 states: "A false balance is an abomination to the Lord, but a just weight is his delight". Deuteronomy 25:13-16 goes into details about the importance of providing proper weights:

> Thou shalt not have in thy bag divers weights, a great and a small:
> thou shalt not have in thine house divers measures, a great and a small:
> but thou shalt have a perfect and just weight, a perfect and just measure
> shalt thou have: that thy days may be lengthened in the land which the
> LORD thy God giveth thee. or all that do such things, and all that do
> unrighteously, are an abomination unto the LORD thy God

Similarly, the Mishnah Torah states the following: "When a person sells an item to a colleague by measure, by weight or by number, and errs to the slightest degree, the colleague may seek redress at any time".[cxxv] Note that the text provides for no statute of limitations – if someone uses improper weights, the person can always be punished.

Additionally, the Talmud (61b) states that "a man is forbidden to keep in his house a measuring vessel smaller or larger than the standard measure even if it is to be used a chamber pot." False weights were of paramount importance for the rabbis. One of the many issues is that a merchant could cause damage to numerous customers by having incorrect prices. It could actually be "virtually impossible to make restitution because of the large number of people involved. [cxxvi]

Instead of measuring weights via a chamber pot, modern companies measure revenue in dollars and cents. Measuring revenue, costs, and other metrics remains extremely important in the modern business environment. People and businesses will give loans very much based on a company's financial condition – it is imperative to have valid information about revenue, costs and other elements. For example, a bank would loan money based on a company's income. An investor would buy or sell stock based on the net income and other factors (e.g., cash flow).

Accounting principles provide the framework that shows the methods that a company must use to make proper financial measurements. Ultimately, a company must provide information about profits or loss, of revenues and expenses, assets the company owns and liability the company owes to others. Generally Accepted Accounting Principles (GAAP) delineates rules to try to show proper information. The importance of providing valid information includes the requirement that publicly traded companies in the United States have an audited financial statement – a company creates a financial statement that lists revenue and expenses, assets owned, and other data. An accounting firm will then review the data to make sure the financial data is accurate. For example, the accounting firm of Ernst & Young would validate that Walmart's net profit of $14.6 billion was accurate.

Ethical scandals have occurred when companies cannot or intentionally will not properly measure the losses and gains, and provide inaccurate data. As people buy and sell stock and make loans based on financial information, the invalid data causes numerous negative downstream impacts.

One upsetting example of not having proper weights was at an accounting firm. An employee had just passed the CPA exam. The employee, a manager, asked a staff member for answers – to the ethics exam (in order to get a CPA, a candidate must past four very difficult exams, and then pass a take-home ethics exam)!! The employee refused to provide the answers to the ex-manager.

Modern regulations are complete with rules to try to avoid a conflict of interest. For example, CPAs who audit (review the financial data to assess accuracy) an entity must not own stock in the company, work in the company or have other relationships that may impair (or seem to impair) judgements. A federal employee who helps to award a contract should not work for the contractor. Many federal employees must sign a form to show all assets owned and positions held.

Epilogue – Additional Overall Notes

i.   Rationalizing Rather than Making Rational Decisions

It is important to understand overall frameworks (as well as specific guidelines). One overriding framework for determining motivation to act maliciously is the fraud triangle[7]. The triangle consists of three parts, with a pneumonic of "PRO" – Pressures [Incentive], Rationalization, and Opportunities[cxxvii]. The fraud triangle demonstrates the importance (and risk) of rationalization.

The fraud triangle can be applied to many ethical decisions. We should consider whenever making important decisions the following: – are we making decisions based on various financial and other pressures, the assumption that we won't get caught, and then the rationalization that our decisions are truly the right thing to do?

One of the highest pressures is to meet shareholder desires – to do whatever is possible to increase the share price: A CEO of a large company said: "As long as the music is playing, you've got to get up and dance." The CEO was referring to the leveraged buyout market in 2007. Before the collapse, there was intense pressure for managers to join in on the huge and risky profits, despite the evident bubbliness of the market."[cxxviii]

An example of an unethical decision is "ghosting" hours – this is when an employee works more hours than the employee indicates on a timesheet. For example, an employee working on an audit had tight deadlines, and must complete audit work in a limited number of hours. The auditor's manager told the auditor to complete the audit in XX hours. The auditor has pressure to meet deadlines. The auditor would ghost hours. The auditor might rationalize that the auditor is "getting the work done…… in fact [the auditor] is going above and beyond of what is required of them." The auditor would rationalize that completing all required steps thoroughly would result in no immediate pay or recognition. The auditor may have the opportunity to ghost hours, as the auditor may work in a firm where the auditor's work is not carefully scrutinized. For example, an auditor's manager could be in different location than the auditor on some days.[cxxix]

Another example of the fraud triangle is the first story of mankind, Adam & Eve. G-d provided a bounty of food and shelter, asking only that mankind not eat from one tree. In one of the first sections in the first part of the Bible, the first woman (Eve) ate from the tree

---

[7] Other scholars have created a "Fraud Diamond" that includes capability. This is where someone would have the "necessary traits and abilities to be the right person to pull it off" and the person has "recognized this particular fraud opportunity and can turn it into reality." As this book focuses on methods an individual can avoid fraud, this book will focus on the fraud triangle. Source is the *CPA Journal*, December 2004. Wolfe, David J and Hemanson, Dana. *2004* http://wweb.uta.edu/faculty/subraman/EMBA-FTW2009/Articles/Fraud%20Diamond%20Four%20Elements.CPAJ2004.pdf – accessed June 16, 2016.

of life, the only thing she was asked not to do. A serpent manipulatively recommended that Eve eat from the tree of life. Eve gave into "peer pressure", and the serpent's advice, which included rationalization and motivation/pressure (go with 3:4 and 3:12-13), Hashem banished Adam and Even from the garden.

Rationalization is an easy and yet detrimental coping mechanism. A company owner might make a decision to increase profits or decrease work effort, and rationalize the decision. In fact, "when people's actions differ from their morals, they begin to rationalize both to protect themselves from a painful contradiction and to build up protection against accusations."[cxxx] Rationalization is probably therefore one of the important parts of the fraud triangle.

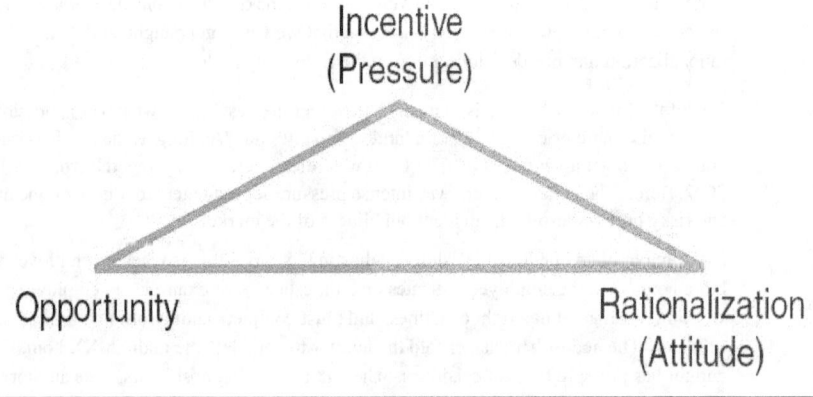

Incentive
(Pressure)

Opportunity

Rationalization
(Attitude)

ii. Porter Lawler – Leading to Bad Behavior

Another important framework to ethical, or lack of ethical, decision making is Porter Lawler. See the chart below.

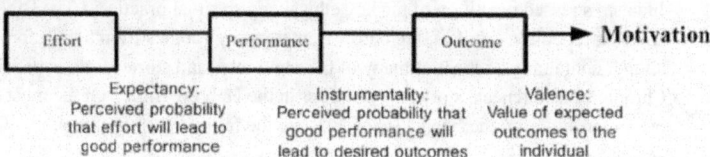

Note: Adapted from http://faculty.css.edu/dswenson/web/OB/VIEtheory.html

Basically, employees will be motivated by believing that if they work hard enough (effort), they will have successful results, which will lead to proper remuneration (e.g., salary)[cxxxi].

The importance of the theory is twofold:

-The employer should realize the importance of providing proper salary, benefits, and work/life balance to employees. If employees perceive the salary/benefits is too low, it is possible the employee may be more likely to steal or do less work to create a feeling of equity.

-The employees should recognize when they are truly rationalizing a lack of work or even taking supplies, and try to understand that they are doing the wrong action, and hopefully be able to change their actions.

iii.   Repetition of Ethical Values

Judaism stressed repetition of the key ethical and spiritual practices. The Bible itself contains repetition – in fact, the book "Deuteronomy" comes from a term for second telling, containing a repeat of many of the same rules and stories from earlier in the bible. Chronicles also repeats stories from earlier in the Hebrew Bible Of the most important prayers in Judaism, the Shema (to hear), state the following in Deuteronomy Chapter 6, versus 6-9.

> And these words, which I command thee this day, shall be in thine heart:

> and thou shalt teach them diligently unto thy children, and shalt talk of them when thou sittest in thine house, and when thou walkest by the way, and when thou liest down, and when thou risest up.

> And thou shalt bind them for a sign upon thine hand, and they shall be as frontlets between thine eyes.

> And thou shalt write them upon the posts of thy house, and on thy gates

Jews are instructed to read the same prayer every morning, and every evening. This prayer is in a ritual item that is in and on the door post of houses (the mezuzah).

Another import part of prayer is Keva, repetition. There are two major facets of prayer: 1) Kavanah (loosely translated as spirit/intention of the prayer), and 2) Keva – repetition. Some believe that both are needed, one to pray often, and to pray with fervor and passion.

This idea of repetition is also important for businesses millennia later. For example, it is helpful for a business to repeat policies on business ethics – not just have employees a brief statement on the employee's first day. Businesses and other entities should learn the importance of repeating the ethical rules, be it via email, web site updates, Twitter, Facebook, or voice mail, or meetings.

iv.   Overall Guidance - No One is Perfect

What do the Biblical Noah, Moses, Jacob, and David have in common? They all made major mistakes. One of the consistent themes of the Hebrew Bible is that most of the major characters have significant shortcomings – all are fallible. It also makes the characters more relatable, and probably a reason that the stories have stood the test of time. [cxxxii]

For example, Noah drank too much and got drunk at inappropriate times. Abraham lied about being married, stating that his wife was his sister in Genesis 20:12. Jacob lied to his father about his birthright, telling his elderly father Isaac that he (Jacob) was Esau. King David, who is actually the forefather of the messiah, found a woman (other than his wife) very attractive. David had relations with her, and she got pregnant. He then put the woman's husband (Uriah) on the front-line so that Uriah would die, and Uriah died in a war (2 Samuel 11:2-17).

This book contains numerous recommendations for proper ethical business practice. The advice can help people in all walks of commerce make better ethical decisions. At the same point, people may not follow the guidance. Managers, employees and consumers will take the road that is easier, that will provide more benefits, and/or that will require less effort. This is human nature (hence Rabbis promulgated various rules to counteract the human instinct, which can be selfish). So if we make mistakes, we must realize that we are only human and have the ability the change (see chapter 24 on Teshuvah).

v.   Though Shalt Teach Business Ethics

One of the most important prayers in Judaism is in a passage from Deuteronomy Chapter 6, Verse 6, which states the importance of teaching to one's child. From this, the Hebrew Bible helps to show the importance of teaching values to children, including business ethics. We can also teach in other roles, as teachers/professors, coaches and boy scout leaders, etc.

We have the ability to teach proper ethics, by stating basic rules, principles, to our children, our siblings, and others in our community. With the internet and social media, we have even more opportunities. We have Twitter, Facebook, and other sites. We have the ability to make comments on stories, which actually can be used for good, not for pernicious gossip, idle online chatter, and insignificant arguments.

vi. Ethics v. Profit

The advice in this book is focused on ethical acts. If an organization follows the rules of this book, the organizations is not guaranteed profit or other prosperity – though avoiding stealing or bribes, as well as accurately reporting financial data, could help an organization avoid fines, horrible publicity, and possible bankruptcy. For example, many companies experienced financial stress, bad publicity and bankruptcy by intentionally falsifying data – WorldCom is one of many examples.

Sometimes, what is good ethically may simply not be good for profit. Sacrifices might be needed to provide employees a better work-life balance, provide more jobs to more people, truly help the environment, or help the community.

vii.   Human Error and Ethics

While there are many important ethical principles, as well as laws and regulations, it is ultimately up to the owners, consumers, vendors and other business practitioners to make the right decision. The Bible and Talmud, as well as other texts have a great deal of leeway, and realize that one ultimately needs to show judgment in making ethical decisions.

Plato said it best:

> "Good people do not need laws to tell them to act responsibly, while bad people will find a way around the laws." [cxxxiii]

An example would be a situation in which El AL, the Israeli airline, due to a computer glitch, listed the incorrect price for a trip. The price for a trip from Israel to the US was only a third of the usual price. Many people bought the tickets. There were numerous Halachah opinions showing either whether one should buy the tickets, or to return the money. The following statement illustrates the important of the spirit of the law:

> "Is there an obligation of going beyond the letter of the law here and return it anyway?" It is this author's [of the article cited] opinion it is recommended that one go beyond the letter of the law when there are individuals who would undergo financial distress in such circumstances. Here, however, each individual should make the choice himself. [cxxxiv]

Ultimately, guidelines can only help so much, as the individuals must make their own decisions.

viii.   Interpreting the Text

While in some cases, the Torah and the Rabbis are fairly clear about rules (e.g., providing prompt payment); in other cases the Rabbis have numerous divergent opinions. This includes rules on business, especially for modern issues. There can be numerous other interpretations and recommendations based on millennia of texts. For example, two Rabbis, Hillel and Shamai had many different opinions about numerous topics. In Judaism today, the Reform, Reconstructionist, Orthodox and Conservative movements will have different interpretations and practice. The guidance in this book, therefore, represents one interpretation of the Torah and Rabbinical rules. There could be other interpretations.

ix.   Reason for 36 Chapters

In Hebrew (the language Jews use in prayer, as well as the language of modern Israel) letters stand for numbers. The first letter, for example, Aleph, is for a 1, the second letter, Vet (Bet) is for 2, etc. The word for Chai, a combination of two letters for 10 + 8 is the word for life. Many Jews gives gifts (e.g., for a wedding, bar mitzvah, bris or charity) in multiples of 18. Therefore, this book provides 36 lessons, two times life.

Why two?

Ultimately, a business transaction requires (at least) two parties such as the buyer and the seller; employee and employer. Business arrangements are a key part of life, providing consumers products they need or desire, providing jobs that give the employees money (not only when employed, but also during retirement) to feed, clothe and house their family. Therefore, this book contains 2 x 18 = 36 chapters.

x.   Annotated Bibliography

This book cites numerous sources, including passages of the Torah, Talmud and other important texts, other books that provide detailed explanations of Jewish law, and many magazines and web sites. Following are several works that can provide further guidance.

The Bible

Of course, one of the most important sources of Jewish business ethics is the Bible itself. The Hebrew Bible is known as the Tanakh – this is an acronym for the Torah, Nevi'im (prophets) and Ketuvim (the Writings, including Chronicles, Proverbs and Psalms). There are numerous translations of the Bible (originally written in Hebrew, as well as other Middle Eastern languages, such as the Aramaic) over the millennia. Of the most famous and classic interpretations was the King James Bible, now freely available on the internet at http://www.bartleby.com/108/.

Mishneh Torah

This is a very important book from Moses ben Maimon (Maimonides), one of the most influential Rabbis. The Chabad (a group of Orthodox Jews) has a website with a link to the full Mishneh Torah. The Mishneh Torah is a listing of various Jewish laws (Halachah):

> The *Mishneh Torah* (literally, "Review of the Torah") was conceived as an all-inclusive halakhic compendium, a guide to the entire system of Jewish law. Maimonides was explicit about his reasons for undertaking an encyclopedic work of such magnitude. He noted that the trials and tribulations of life in the Diaspora had deprived scholars and laymen alike of the ability to understand and assimilate the vast talmudic literature and the essential rulings of the *geonim* (the leaders of Babylonian and North African Jewry); consequently, Jews were unable to discern or properly observe the law. In its comprehensive scope, its pragmatic style, and its classification, the *Mishneh Torah* was designed to simplify the process of study and to make the law accessible to all.[cxxxv]

The following site is a link to the book of Mechirah (laws of selling) within the Mishneh Torah: http://www.chabad.org/library/article_cdo/aid/1362849/jewish/Mechirah.htm.

Talmud

Another important book is the Talmud, which is a combination of laws and stories, including the Mishnah (a book that Rabbis redacted around 200 of the Common Era (CE, what others call AD), and the Gemara (this is a large series of stories and rules that Rabbis wrote from 200 C.E. to 500 C.E. There are Babylonian and Jerusalem versions[cxxxvi]).

The following is a link to a section about financial claims of two people.

http://www.come-and-hear.com/babamezia/

Business Halacha

This is a thorough book that provides very detailed rules about Jewish rules about business ethics. This book contains forms that can be used to create contracts and lists many rules and regulations. *Business Halacha* has been very helpful in writing this book.

Values, Prosperity and the Talmud

Values, Prosperity and the Talmud is an excellent book, providing some information about Jewish teachings, as well as helpful anecdotes. This book contains many examples of modern businesses.

xi.   Acknowledgements

This book is the result of almost four decades of learning, from the classroom to the boardroom to the temple. I have learned the theory of proper ethics, seen how businesses actually run, and researched employer's decisions.

I would like to thank my professors at the McIntire School of Commerce at the University of Virginia and the Robert H Smith School of Business at the University of Maryland for providing me information about various ethical guidelines on running a business, as well as scholarly information about religions (I minored in religious studies at UVA). I would also like to thank my fellow faculty, administration, and students at the University of Maryland University College (UMUC) from their important insight and scholarship.

Thanks to my numerous managers I have had in my 17 years of professional work, from consulting to government service, teaching to coaching. I have had seven employers from full-time positions, as well as other employers (e.g., UMUC and Becker CPA Review) for part-time positions. From each of my colleagues, managers, and business associates, I have gleaned lessons on how companies, managers and employees can decide to run a business and make decisions on hiring, promoting and managing people and projects.

Thank you for the study partner from Partners in Torah, Avram Rosenberg. We studied *Business Halachah* for many months, and I appreciate his important insight.

Thanks for the numerous resources that provided me helpful information, especially to Chabad, Artscroll/Rabbi Ari Marburger, Larry Kahaner, and Mozniam Publications / Rabbi Eliyahu Touger.

I want to thank Mom and Dad, Jacob and Sandra Kaufman, for teaching about proper ethical practices, providing examples on how to manage a business and employees, and showing how to ethically work. Thank you for supporting me to obtain an education, both in the classroom and the temple. I continue to learn from you.

Thank you to my wife, Rachelle Kaufman, for teaching me about business ethics, from running her own businesses to important insight about her business dealings, to her commentary about various corporations. She shows integrity in her business and everything she does. Her hard work and perseverance in publishing her numerous books (Kaufman Green Guides) has helped motivate me to finish this book. She also has edited this book. Thank you to my son, Benjamin – though you are now a newborn and can't read the book at this point, you provided inspiration and a new perspective (as your father) as I made additional edits to this book. [8]

---

[8] I wrote this version in 2016, after the birth of my son. I published the original edition in 2015.

xii.   Bio

Noah Kaufman is a systems accountant/project manager. He has worked as an accountant for over 17 years, including working for federal agencies since 2009. He has held several management positions, including in financial reporting, financial systems and financial policy. He worked for several years in consulting, including as a Senior Consultant. He began his career in public accounting, working for Arthur Andersen.

He received his BS in 1999 from the University of Virginia, with a minor in Religious Studies, and got an MBA from the University of Maryland. He is a CPA, CGFM and CGMA. He is an Associate Adjunct Professor at UMUC, teaching classes in federal financial management, taxation, accounting software, and financial systems. He also taught Intermediate Accounting at UVA for several years. Additionally, he teaches at Becker CPA review, where he has taught classes and prepared other educational materials.

He has coached High School / Youth wrestling for over 17 years, including fifteen years at George C Marshall High School in Falls Church, VA.

Mr. Kaufman has written several books, including *Lessons from the Wresting Mat - Life Lessons from a Quarter Century of Coaching and Competing.* He has published other materials, including a letter to the editor in a government accounting magazine and several articles in a state accounting journal. He has also presented at conferences, including at the 2015 AICPA Not-for-Profit Conference. He lives in the DC area with his wife, son, and a cat. He was also born and raised in Northern Virginia, near Washington, DC.

Picture taken by Lauren Fassler.

2l2222222222222222222222222

[i] Marburer, Rabbi Ari. *Business Halacha*. Brooklyn, NY: Mesorah Publications, LTD. 2008. Print. This (and other quotes in this book) Reproduced from Business Halacha by Rabbi Ari Marburger with permission of the copyright holders, ArtScroll / Mesorah Publications, Ltd.

[ii] Kahaner, Larry. *Values, Prosperities and the Talmud*. Hoboken, New Jersey: John Wiley & Sons, Inc. 2003. Print. *Note – thank you for the email consent to publish the quotes from the book.*

[iii] Ibid. (Page 4).

[iv] Marburer, Rabbi Ari. *Business Halacha*. Brooklyn, NY: Mesorah Publications, LTD. 2008. Print.

[v] King James translation. Web. Nd. <http://www.bartleby.com/108/03/>. These and other quotes are for the same site.

[vi] Harjani, Ansuya. "Shoplifting cost the world $112 billion last year. "13 Nov 2013. *CNBC*. <http://www.cnbc.com/id/101193427>. Web. 2 July 2015.

[vii] McCrabb, Rick. "Theft from retail centers costs shoppers, stores." 5 Sept 2013. *Dayton Daily News*. Web. <http://www.daytondailynews.com/news/news/theft-from-retail-centers-costs-shoppers-stores/nZmxy/>. 2 July 2015.

[viii] Kahaner, Larry. *Values, Prosperities and the Talmud*. Hoboken, New Jersey: John Wiley & Sons, Inc. 2003. Print.

[ix] Birnbaum, Jordanna. "Shomer Negia." Nd. *My Jewish Learning*. Web. <http://www.myjewishlearning.com/article/shomer-negiah>. 3 July 2015.

[x] "Law and Business Ethics." *On1Foot: Jewish Texts for Social Justice (American Jewish World Service)*. Nd. Web. <http://www.on1foot.org/taxonomy/term/54?tid%5B%5D=20&field_source_value_many_to_one%5B%5D=Medieval+%28Geonim+through+the+16th+Century%29>. 5 July 2015.

[xi] "Foreign National Convicted in Multi-Million-Dollar, Multi-State Criminal Operation." *FBI. 4 March 2013*. Web. <http://www.fbi.gov/houston/press-releases/2013/foreign-national-convicted-in-multi-million-dollar-multi-state-criminal-operation>. 14 July 2015.

[xii] Yiannopoulos, Milo. "How Reddit Supports Trade in Stolen Goods, in Plain Sight of the Internet." *Breitbart*. 25 Sep 2014. Web. <http://www.breitbart.com/Breitbart-London/2014/09/25/How-Reddit-supports-trade-in-stolen-goods-in-plain-sight-of-the-internet>. 19 July 2015.

[xiii] "18 U.S. Code § 2315 - Sale or receipt of stolen goods, securities, moneys, or fraudulent State tax stamps." *Cornell University Law School (Legal Information Institute*. Nd. Web. <http://www.law.cornell.edu/uscode/text/18/2315>. 19 July 2015.

[xiv] "As if you needed another reason to hate Metallica." *Techspot*. 17 Jul 2003. Web. <http://www.techspot.com/community/topics/as-if-you-needed-another-reason-to-hate-metallica.6423/> 19 July 2015.

[xv] Wilson, Jeffrey. "The 10 Most-Pirated Movies. 14 July 2015. *PC*. Web. <http://www.pcmag.com/slideshow/story/315170/the-10-most-pirated-movies?ipmat=327460&ipmtype=5>. 19 July 2015. *Author's note – I have seen three of the movies from a list on September 16, 2014, including "Divergent." A Million Ways to Die in the West, and the "Giver".*

[xvi] Neusner, Jacob. *The Mishnah: A New Translation*. New Haven and London: Yale University Press. 1988. Print.

[xvii] Deuteronomy 11:19. King James translation. <http://www.bartleby.com/108/05/11.html#19>. 3 July 2015. *Note – other Bible quotes are from the King James translation, from the same website, at* http://www.bartleby.com/108

[xviii] Kahaner, Larry. *Values, Prosperities and the Talmud*. Hoboken, New Jersey: John Wiley & Sons, Inc. 2003. Print.

[xix] "Talmud - Mas. Kiddushin 29a." *Halakhah.com*. Web. http://halakhah.com/pdf/nashim/Kiddushin.pdf. 19 July 2015.

[xx] Kavoussi, Bonnie. "Half Of Recent College Graduates Lack Full-Time Job, Study Says." 10 May 2012. *Huffington Post*. Web. <http://www.huffingtonpost.com/2012/05/10/college-graduates-full-time-jobs-

study_n_1496827.html>. 19 July 2015.

xxi"College Graduates Struggle to Find Employment Worth a Degree." 5 Jun 2014. *NewsMax*. Web. <http://www.newsmax.com/US/college-graduates-jobs/2014/06/05/id/575299/>. 19 July 2015.

xxii"An economy that works: Job creation and America's future." June 2011. *McKinsey Global Institute (McKinsey & Company)*. Web. <http://www.mckinsey.com/insights/employment_and_growth/an_economy_that_works_for_us_job_creation>. 19 July 2015.

xxiii "Babylonian Talmud: Tractate Nedarim / Folio 49a / CHAPTER VI." Nd. *Come and Hear*. Web. <http://www.come-and-hear.com/nedarim/nedarim_49.html>. 20 July 2015. Immigrant America: The Worst Job in New York

xxivTucker, Rabbi Gordon. "The Dignity of Work and the Indignity of Slavery." Nd. T'ruah. Web. <http://www.truah.org/documents/Dignity-of-work.pdf>. 20 July 2015.

xxv Kahaner, Larry. *Values, Prosperities and the Talmud*. Hoboken, New Jersey: John Wiley & Sons, Inc. 2003. Print.

xxvi Smith, Greg. "Head Coach Steve Masiello Loses $5M For Lying on Resume." 31 August 2014. BlackSportsOnline (GSO). Web. <http://blacksportsonline.com/home/2014/03/head-coach-steve-masiello-loses-5m-for-lying-on-resume/> 20 July 2015.

xxvii "Wal-Mart Spokesman Said to Resign Over Falsehood in His Resume." 16 Sep 2014. *Newsmax*. Web. < http://www.newsmax.com/finance/Companies/Wal-Mart-Spokesman-Falsehood-Resume/2014/09/16/id/594918/> . 20 Jul 2015.

xxviiiFastenberg, Dan. "The Most Common Lies On Resumes." 1 Apr 2013. *AOL*. Web. <http://jobs.aol.com/articles/2013/04/01/common-lies-resumes/> 20 Jul 2015.

xxix Citron, Aryeh. "The Mitzvah of Giving Loans (Parshat Re'eh)." Nd. *Chabad.Org*. Web. < http://www.chabad.org/library/article_cdo/aid/957872/jewish/The-Mitzvah-of-Giving-Loans.htm#footnote1a957872.> 20 Jul 2015. Reprinted with permission from Chabad.org.

xxx Kahaner, Larry. *Values, Prosperities and the Talmud*. Hoboken, New Jersey: John Wiley & Sons, Inc. 2003. Print. (Kahaner is quoting from Ketubot, 50a).

xxxi Ibid (Page 148).

xxxii Ibid (Pages 209-210).

xxxiii Harris, Jennie. *Toastmaster*. May 2015. Page 29. Print.

xxxiv Dewanoct, Shaila. "Microcredit for Americans." 28 Oct 2013. *New York Times*. Web. <http://www.nytimes.com/2013/10/29/business/microcredit-for-americans.html?_r=0>. 20 Jul 2015.

xxxv Hughes, Kim. "Whole Foods Foundation's Micro-Loans Help 1.3 Million People." SamaritanMag. 12 Nov 2012. *SamaritanMag.com*. Web. <http://www.samaritanmag.com/1427/whole-foods-foundations-micro-loans-help-13-million-people>. 20 Jul 2015.

xxxvi Kahaner, Larry. *Values, Prosperities and the Talmud*. Hoboken, New Jersey: John Wiley & Sons, Inc. 2003. Print.

xxxvi Marburer, Rabbi Ari. *Business Halacha*. Brooklyn, NY: Mesorah Publications, LTD. 2008. Print.

xxxvii "Jewish Principles in the Workplace: A Money and Morals Guide." *Jewish Association for Business Ethics*. Nd. Web. < http://www.scojec.org/resources/files/workplace_ethics.pdf> 5 July 2015.

xxxixDrury, Ian. "Snowden leaks cost lives, say terror experts: Extremists 'changed their tactics after fugitive's leaks about intelligence operations.'" 26 Nov 2014. *Daily Mail.com* Web. http://www.dailymail.co.uk/news/article-2849605/Snowden-leaks-cost-lives-say-terror-experts-Extremists-changed-tactics-fugitives-leaks-intelligence-operations.html?ITO=1490&ns_mchannel=rss&ns_campaign=1490. 21 Jul 2015.

xl Kahaner, Larry. *Values, Prosperities and the Talmud*. Hoboken, New Jersey: John Wiley & Sons, Inc. 2003. Print.

xli Trottman, Melanie. "Facebook Firing Case is Settled." *Wall Street Journal*. 8 February 2011. <http://www.wsj.com/articles/SB10001424052748704422204576130631738779412>. 6 June 2015.

xliiBotbol, Isaac. "Leadership and the Hispanic Supervisor." Nd. *Training for Hispanics in the Workplace*. Web. <http://trainingforhispanics.com/leadership-and-the-hispanic-supervisor/>. 21 Jul 2015.

[xliii] Bruzzese, Anita. "Trash Talking the Boss." 8 Feb 2011. *45 Things.* Web. <http://onthejob.45things.com/2011/02/trash-talking-boss.html>. 21 Jul 2015.

[xliv] Kahaner, Larry. *Values, Prosperities and the Talmud.* Hoboken, New Jersey: John Wiley & Sons, Inc. 2003. Print.

[xlv] Marburer, Rabbi Ari. *Business Halacha.* Brooklyn, NY: Mesorah Publications, LTD. 2008. Print.

[xlvi]"Promises and Rescinded Job Offers." Nd. *Lawyers.com.* Web. <http://labor-employment-law.lawyers.com/Job-Hunting/Promises-and-Rescinded-Job-Offers.html>. 21 Jul 2015.

[xlvii] Zaretsky, Staci. "Which Biglaw Firm Is Rescinding Offers?" 14 Apr 2014. *Above the Law.* Web. <http://abovethelaw.com/2014/04/which-biglaw-firm-is-rescinding-offers/>. 21 Jul 2015.

[xlviii] "Jewish Principles in the Workplace." Nd. *Jewish association for business ethics.* Web. <http://www.jabe.org/userfiles/publications/JABE%20Jewish%20Principles%20in%20the%20Workplace%20-%20Email%20Version.pdf>. 21 Jul 2015.

[xlix] Brooks, Mark S and Kenney, Andrew. "Collision Course to Collaboration." *CGMA Magazine.* June 2016. Page 27. Print.

[l] Ibid.

[li] Kahaner, Larry. *Values, Prosperities and the Talmud.* Hoboken, New Jersey: John Wiley & Sons, Inc. 2003. Print.

[lii] Mohl, Nachum. "Comforting the Poor." *The Jewish Magazine.* July 2008. Web. <http://www.jewishmag.com/125mag/comforting_poor/comforting_poor.htm>. 4 June 2015.

[liii] "Reasons I Joined Accenture #5 – Giving something back." 12 May 2014. *Accenture* (Accenture.com). Web. 23 Nov 23, 2014.

[liv] Kahaner, Larry. *Values, Prosperities and the Talmud.* Hoboken, New Jersey: John Wiley & Sons, Inc. 2003. Print.

[lv] Ibid (Page 214).

[lvi] Pfeffer, Harav Yehoshua. "Kedoshim – How to Pay Workers." 27 Apr 2011 [23 Nisan 5771 on site]. *DIN – The International Beis Horah.* Web <http://www.dinonline.org/2011/04/27/how-to-pay-workers/> 21 Jul 2015.

[lvii] Ibid.

[lviii] Marburer, Rabbi Ari. *Business Halacha.* Brooklyn, NY: Mesorah Publications, LTD. 2008. Print.

[lix] Ibid.

[lx] Eichler, Alexander. "Working Poor: Almost Half Of U.S. Households Live One Crisis From The Bread Line." 31 Jan 2012. *The Huffington Post.* Web. <http://www.huffingtonpost.com/2012/01/31/working-poor-liquid-asset-poverty_n_1243152.html>. 22 Jul 2015.

[lxi] "Food bank helps furloughed Grand Canyon workers as business owners protest closure." 9 Oct 013. *Fox News.* Web. <http://www.foxnews.com/politics/2013/10/09/grand-canyon-workers-stranded-without-food-amid-slimdown/>. 22 Jul 2015.

[lxii] "Public Law 97-177 –May 21, 1982." *Government Printing Office (GPO).* Web. <http://www.gpo.gov/fdsys/pkg/STATUTE-96/pdf/STATUTE-96-Pg85.pdf> 22 Jul 2015.

[lxiii] "Prompt Payment." Nd. *US Department of Treasury.* Web. <http://fms.treas.gov/prompt/ftr.pdf>. Accessed on 12 31 2013.

[lxiv] "§ 2.2-4352. Prompt payment of bills by localities." n.d. *Commonwealth of Virginia.* Web. <http://leg1.state.va.us/cgi-bin/legp504.exe?000+cod+2.2-4352>. 22 Jul 2015.

[lxv] "§ 2.2-4355. Interest penalty; exceptions." n.d. *Law Server.* Web. <https://www.lawserver.com/law/state/virginia/va-code/virginia_code_2-2-4355> 22 Jul 2015.

[lxvi] Kahaner, Larry. *Values, Prosperities and the Talmud.* Hoboken, New Jersey: John Wiley & Sons, Inc. 2003. Print.

[lxvii] Gilpin, Kenneth. "Ex Sunbeam Executives to pay 15 million to settle a lawsuit." *New York Times.* 15 January 2002. Web. <http://www.nytimes.com/2002/01/15/business/ex-sunbeam-executives-to-pay-15-million-to-settle-a-lawsuit.html> 6 June 2015.

[lxviii] Kahaner, Larry. *Values, Prosperities and the Talmud.* Hoboken, New Jersey: John Wiley & Sons, Inc. 2003. Print.

lxix Amato, Neil (As told to Neil Amato [interview with Steve Watson, CFO of the Biltmore Estates)). "The Last Word." *AICPA Journal of Accountancy.* May 2014. Page 80. Print.

lxx Khazan, Olga. "Life in the Sickest Town in America." 22 Jan 2015. *The Atlantic.* Web. <http://www.theatlantic.com/features/archive/2015/01/life-in-the-sickest-town-in-america/384718/>. 22 Jul 2015.

lxxi "EB-5 Immigrant Investor." *n.d.* Department of Homeland Security / US Citizenship and Immigration Services. *Web.* <http://www.uscis.gov/eb-5> 22 Jul 2015.

lxxii Kahaner, Larry. *Values, Prosperities and the Talmud.* Hoboken, New Jersey: John Wiley & Sons, Inc. 2003. Print.

lxxiii "Mechirah - Chapter Eighteen." Translated by Eliyahu Touger. n.d. *Chabad.* <http://www.chabad.org/library/article_cdo/aid/1363957/jewish/Mechirah-Chapter-Eighteen.htm>. 22 Jul 2015. *Note –this quote, and others from the Mechirah are from a Mishneh Torah translation published by Moznaim publications; permission provided by the Moznaim publications.* The physical book can be purchased at http://www.moznaim.com/mishneh-torah-2508.html.

lxxiv Marburer, Rabbi Ari. *Business Halacha.* Brooklyn, NY: Mesorah Publications, LTD. 2008. Print.

lxxv Ibid. Page 203.

lxxviKahaner, Larry. *Values, Prosperities and the Talmud.* Hoboken, New Jersey: John Wiley & Sons, Inc. 2003. Print.

lxxvii"Babylonian Talmud: Tractate Baba Mezi'a / Bava Mezia 77b."" n.d. *Come and Hear.* Web. <http://www.come-and-hear.com/babamezia/babamezia_77.html>. 23 Jul 2015.

lxxviii "Pay and Leave." n.d. *OPM (U.S. Office of Personnel Management).* Web. <http://www.opm.gov/policy-data-oversight/pay-leave/leave-administration/fact-sheets/leave-for-funerals-and-bereavement/>. 23 Jul 2015.

lxxix "Jewish Principles in the Workplace." n.d. *Jewish Association for Business Ethics.* Web. <http://www.jabe.org/userfiles/publications/JABE%20Jewish%20Principles%20in%20the%20Workplace%20-%20Email%20Version.pdf>. 21 Jul 2015.

lxxx Cooper, Rabbi Fredi. "Preparing for a Rabbinic Sabbatical From the Perspective of the Congregational Leadership." n.d. *Jewish Reconstructionist Communities.* Web. http://www.jewishrecon.org/resource/preparing-rabbinic-sabbatical-perspective-congregational-leadership. 25 Jul 2015.

lxxxi Pagano, Elizabeth and Pagaono. "The Virtues and Challenges of a Long Break." Feb 2009. *(AICPA) Journal of Accountancy.* Web. <http://www.journalofaccountancy.com/Issues/2009/Feb/VirtuesAndChallenges.htm>. 30 Nov 2013.

lxxxii Dalphonse, Sherri. "50 best places to work". Dec 2013. *Washingtonian.* Page 77. Print.

lxxxiii Adams, Susan. "13 American Companies With Remarkable Perks." n.d. *Forbes.* Web. <http://www3.forbes.com/leadership/13-american-companies-with-remarkable-perks/3/>. 25 2015.

lxxxiv Salvatore Babones. "Fair Work, Fair Pay: Lessons From Australia". 26 Dec 2011. *Truthout.* Web <http://truth-out.org/opinion/item/5601> 23 Jul 2015.

lxxxv "Fair Trade Principles and Jewish Values." Jul 2011. *Fair Trade Judaica.* Web. < http://fairtradejudaica.org/wp-content/uploads/2011/07/FairTradeJewishValuesMatrix.pdf> 23 Jul 2015. (Note – translation in section for "Support Community Development & Sustainability".)

lxxxviMeir, Rabbi Dr. Asher (Business Ethics Center of Jerusalem). "The Jewish Ethicist: Showing Racism the Door Should I fire a racist worker?" 7 Aug 2014. *Aish.com.* Web. <http://www.aish.com/ci/be/48891142.html>. 7 June 2015.

lxxxvii Szalavitz, Maia. "Do People Really Drink More When the Economy Tanks?." 17 Oct 2011. *Time.* Web. <http://healthland.time.com/2011/10/17/do-people-really-drink-more-when-the-economy-tanks/#ixzz2dmddmASO>. 24 Jul 2015.

lxxxviii Marburer, Rabbi Ari. *Business Halacha.* Brooklyn, NY: Mesorah Publications, LTD. 2008. Print.

lxxxix Jacobs, Rabbi Louis. "Hillel, the preeminent rabbi of first century Palestine." *My Jewish Learning.* Web.

<http://www.myjewishlearning.com/article/hillel/>. 25 Jul 2015.
[xc] Nayab, N (edited by Scheid, Jean). "10 Common Employer Mistakes That Lead to Employee Lawsuits." 12 Jan 2011. *bright hub*. Web. http://www.brighthub.com/office/human-resources/articles/102686.aspx. 26 Jul 2015.
[xci] Harris, Leon. "What you need to know about severance pay, UK pensions." 31 Aug 2010. *Jerusalem Post*. Web. <http://www.jpost.com/Business/Commentary/What-you-need-to-know-about-severance-pay-UK-pensions>. 26 Jul 2015.
[xcii] Broyde, Rabbi Michael. "Severance Pay and Jewish Law." 30 Jul 2002. *Beth Din of America*. Web. <http://www.bethdin.org/docs/PDF10-Severance_Pay_and_Jewish_Law.pdf>. 26 Jul 2015.
[xciii] Ibid.
[xciv] "Chevra Kadisha." n.d. *Congregation Agudath Sholom* Web. <http://www.congregationagudathsholom.org/chevrakadisha.htm>. 26 Jul 2015.
[xcv] Marburer, Rabbi Ari. *Business Halacha*. Brooklyn, NY: Mesorah Publications, LTD. 2008. Print.
[xcvi] "Tax Refund Loans: Instant Trouble." n.d. *Centre for Responsible Lending*. Web. <http://www.responsiblelending.org/other-consumer-loans/refund-anticipation-loans/>. 26 Jul 2015.
[xcvii] Marburer, Rabbi Ari. Business Halacha. Brooklyn, NY: Mesorah Publications, LTD. 2008. Print
[xcviii] Hoffman, Rabbi Yair. "The Elal Pricing Error: A Halachic Analysis." n.d. *5 Towns Jewish Times*. Web. <http://5tjt.com/the-elal-pricing-error-a-halachic-analysis-by-rabbi-yair-hoffman/>. 26 Jul 2015.
[xcix] Marburer, Rabbi Ari. Business Halacha. Brooklyn, NY: Mesorah Publications, LTD. 2008. Print
[c] Ives, Rabbi Yossi. "Judaism and the Environment." 24 Jan 2014. *Aish*. Web. http://www.aish.com/h/15sh/i/48965876.html > 26 Jul 2015.
[ci] Ibid.
[cii] Schwartz, Richard. "Judaism and Animal Rights." n.d. *JewishVeg.com*. Web. <http://www.jewishveg.com/schwartz/judaism_ar.html>. 31 Jul 2015.
[ciii] "What is Green Kosher" n.d. *Empire Kosher*. Web. <http://www.empirekosher.com/faq/about-empire-kosher/what-is-green-kosher/>. 26 Jul 2015.
[civ] "Mechirah – Chapter Fourteen." Translated by Eliyahu Touger. n.d. *Chabad*. <http://www.chabad.org/library/article_cdo/aid/1363957/jewish/Mechirah-Chapter-Eighteen.htm>. 22 Jul 2015.
[cv] Fallon, Nicole. "Bullying in the Office: Why You Need a Policy." 10 Feb 2014. *Business News Daily*. Web. <http://www.businessnewsdaily.com/5900-workplace-bullying-policy.html>. 27 Jul 2015.
[cvi] Reilly, Peter. "When the Whistle Blows: Successful resolution start with effective policies." May/June 2015. *Disclosures*. Page 25. Print.
[cvii] Castillo, Michelle. "Workplace bullying linked to more antidepressant, tranquilizer use." 18 Dec 2012. *CBS News*. Web. <http://www.cbsnews.com/news/workplace-bullying-linked-to-more-antidepressant-tranquilizer-use/>. 27 Jul 2015.
[cviii] Johnson, Travis. "Workplace Bullying: New Trend Or An Old Problem Gaining Attention?" 6 Feb 2013. *TLNT*. Web. <http://www.tlnt.com/2013/02/06/workplace-bullying-new-trend-or-an-old-problem-gaining-attention/>. 27 Jul 2015.
[cix] Jacobs, Rabbi Jill. "Work, workers and the Jewish owner." n.d. *Rabbinical Assembly*. Web. http://www.rabbinicalassembly.org/sites/default/files/public/halakhah/teshuvot/20052010/jacobs-living-wage.pdf. 27 Jul 2015.
[cx] Ginzberg, Louis. "Legends of the Jews." *Internet Sacred Texts Archive*. Web. <http://www.sacred-texts.com/jud/loj/loj106.htm>. 27 Jul 2015. *Note* - published in 1909, and available on the site.
[cxi] Dorian, Marc, Putrino, Lauren and Valiente, Alexa. " 'Midnight Rider' Hairstylist Describes When Train Hit Her, Killed Fellow Crew Member." 31 Oct 2014. *ABC News*. Web. <http://abcnews.go.com/Entertainment/midnight-rider-hairstylist-describes-horrific-moments-train-hit/story?id=26523394>. 27 Jul 2015.
[cxii] Leggett, Christopher. "The Ford Pinto Case: the Valuation of Life as it Applies to the Negligence-Efficiency Argument." Spring 1999. *Wake Forest University*. Web.

<http://users.wfu.edu/palmitar/Law&Valuation/Papers/1999/Leggett-pinto.html>. 28 Jul 2015.

cxiii "Best Accounting Firms for Work-Life Balance." n.d. *Vault.com*. Web.
<http://www.vault.com/company-rankings/accounting/best-accounting-firms-to-work-for/?sRankID=322&rYear=2015&pg=1>. 28 Jul 2015.

cxiv Bellstrom, Kristen. "EY Comes Out Swinging at Other Consulting Firms With New Parental Leave Policy." 13 Apr 2016. *Fortune*. Web. <http://fortune.com/2016/04/13/ey-parental-leave-policy/>.

cxv "Metro studying fatigue among employees." 7 Dec 2012. *The Daily Record*. Web.
<http://thedailyrecord.com/2012/12/07/metro-studying-fatigue-among-employees/>. 28 Jul 2015. Note – Associated Press article.

cxvi Marburer, Rabbi Ari. *Business Halacha*. Brooklyn, NY: Mesorah Publications, LTD. 2008. Print. *Note -* quotes Shevas Yaakov 3.176.

cxvii Weiss, R. Yosaif Ashe. The Festivals and Days of Awe. Brooklyn, NY: Mesorah Publications, LTD. 2007. Print.

cxviii Hattem, Julian. 22 Oct 2013. "ATM Company to Pay $48 Million to settle bribery charges." *The Hill*. Web. < http://thehill.com/regulation/finance/329891-atm-company-to-pay-48-million-over-bribery-charges->. 28 Jul 2015.

cxixWhitlock, Craig. "Senior officer, NCIS agent are among those arrested in Navy bribery scandal." *The Washington Post*. Web. <http://www.washingtonpost.com/world/national-security/senior-officer-ncis-agent-are-among-those-arrested-in-navy-bribery-scandal/2013/10/19/e9a1e9b6-3753-11e3-bda2-e637e3241dc8_story.html>. 28 Jul 2015.

cxx "AP corrects ethics reform reference in trial story." 5 Sep 2014. *WTOP*. Web.
<http://www.wtop.com/41/3694949/Ex-Virginia-gov-wife-guilty-of-public-corruption#ixzz3CPQI0w7m>. 28 Jul 2015.

cxxi" Corruption on the Rise Globally." October 2013. *Journal of Accountancy*. Web.
<http://www.journalofaccountancy.com/Issues/2013/Oct/20138364> 28 Jul 2015.

cxxii "China hands drugmaker GSK record $489 million fine for paying bribes." 19 Sep 2014. *Yahoo!* Web.
<http://finance.yahoo.com/news/china-fines-gsk-489-million-082944525.html;_ylt=A0LEVvLh9hxUGAsAe6xjmolQ>. 28 Jul 2015.

cxxiii Kahaner, Larry. *Values, Prosperities and the Talmud*. Hoboken, New Jersey: John Wiley & Sons, Inc. 2003. Print.

cxxiv Reh, John. "The Right People in the Wrong Jobs." n.d. *About.com*.
<http://management.about.com/cs/people/a/RightWrong1099.htm>. 29 Jul 2015.

cxxv "Mechirah - Chapter Fifteen." Translated by Eliyahu Touger. n.d. *Chabad*. Web.
<http://www.chabad.org/library/article_cdo/aid/1363957/jewish/Mechirah-Chapter-Eighteen.htm>. 22 Jul 2015.

cxxvi Kahaner, Larry. *Values, Prosperities and the Talmud*. Hoboken, New Jersey: John Wiley & Sons, Inc. 2003. Print.

cxxvii "The Fraud Triangle." n.d. *Association of Certified Fraud Examiners*. Web.
<http://www.acfe.com/fraud-triangle.aspx>. 29 Jul 2015.

cxxviii Nilsen, Max and Groth, Aimee. "27 Psychological Reasons Why Good People Do Bad Things." 27 Aug 2012. *Business Insider*. Web. <http://www.businessinsider.com/27-psychological-reasons-why-good-people-do-bad-things-2012-8?op=1#ixzz2paHxccaR>. 29 Jul 2015.

cxxix Hayes, Arthur A Jr. "Auditors Taking Our Own Advice – Part V". *Journal of Government Financial Management*. Winter 2012. Page 54. Print.

cxxx Nilsen, Max and Groth, Aimee. "27 Psychological Reasons Why Good People Do Bad Things." 27 Aug 2012. *Business Insider*. Web. <http://www.businessinsider.com/27-psychological-reasons-why-good-people-do-bad-things-2012-8?op=1#ixzz2paHxccaR>. 29 Jul 2015.

cxxxi

"Omeihe, Kingsley. "Remunerations&Rewards on Motivation using Porter and Lawler's model of Motivation. 2013. *Academia.edu*. Web.
<http://www.academia.edu/4422535/Remunerations_and_Rewards_on_Motivation_using_Porter_and_La

wlers_model_of_Motivation>. 30 Jul 2015.

[cxxxii] Brown, Rabbi Randy. Ft. Belvoir. 25 November 2013. Sermon.

[cxxxiii] "Plato." *Wisdom Quotes.* n.d. Web <http://www.wisdomquotes.com/authors/plato/>. 30 June 2015.

[cxxxiv] Hoffman, Rabbi Yair. "The Elal Pricing Error: A Halachic Analysis." n.d. *5 Towns Jewish Times.* Web. <http://5tjt.com/the-elal-pricing-error-a-halachic-analysis-by-rabbi-yair-hoffman>. 31 Jul 2015.

[cxxxv] Furst, Rachel. "The Mishneh Torah." Nd. *My Jewish Learning.* Web. <http://www.myjewishlearning.com/article/the-mishneh-torah/>. 25 May 2016.

[cxxxvi] "THE GEMARA." Nd. *NSW Board of Jewish Education.* Web. < http://bje.org.au/course/judaism/jewish-texts/gemara/>. 25 May 2016.